A TRIUMPHANT STORY OF FAITH & PERSEVERANCE

NO SUCH THING -as- Can't

Lisa Sexton & Tyler Sexton, MD

Tyndale House Publishers
Carol Stream, Illinois

FOCUS ON THE FAMILY®

No Such Thing as Can't: A Triumphant Story of Faith and Perseverance

A Focus on the Family book published by Tyndale House Publishers, Carol Stream, Illinois 60188

Editor: Julie B. Holmquist

Cover design: Sally Dunn

For information about special discounts for bulk purchases, please contact Tyndale House Publishers at csresponse@tyndale.com, or call 1-800-323-9400.

ISBN 978-1-58997-973-4

Library of Congress Cataloging-in-Publication Data can be found at www.loc.gov.

Printed in the United States of America

26 25 24 23 22 21 20
7 6 5 4 3 2 1

Contents

1

DREAMS *CAN* COME TRUE

I'm only six years old, but I already know the drill. It usually starts at the family dinner table.

"Eat up, Tyler," my mom tells me. "You can't have any snacks tonight or any breakfast tomorrow. We're going to see the doctor in the morning."

I'm sitting in front of a dish heaped with some of my favorite foods, and Mom is smiling at me. Even though I know I won't be able to have breakfast, I'm too anxious to eat much.

"Hey, Tyler," Dad says. "Are you ready to play Contra after dinner?"

I love that video game, but Dad's offer doesn't make me happy.

"Dad, I don't feel like playing right now," I say, trying to smile.

"I know you must be nervous, Tyler, but playing a game might take your mind off of tomorrow."

"I just *can't*, Dad."

You guys are so faking it, I say to myself, knowing they are doing their best to take my mind off what's happening tomorrow. We have gone through the same motions so many times before. Another surgery. Another night of feeling so scared before another day of fear. And then, after that, a lot of painful physical therapy.

I can't eat or focus on a game. My parents try and try to make me feel better, but it isn't working. I'm just a little kid, and I wish I didn't have cerebral palsy and need operations. At the same time, I know my mom and dad love me and hope that another surgery will help me walk without braces strapped on both my legs.

That night my parents tuck me in bed and say those flowery words parents say when they want their kid to not be afraid.

"Tyler," Mom says as she sits next to me on my bed, "you're so brave, and we know that you'll be doing great by this time tomorrow."

Great? I think to myself. *Sure! Lots of pain and lots of pain and lots of pain.* I don't say any of that as I look at my mom trying so hard to make me feel better.

"Remember, Jesus is with you," she keeps trying. "He'll protect you, and Dad and I and all our friends at church will be praying for you."

"I know," I mumble as my dad walks up next to my mom. Dad now starts to help make me feel better too.

I wish the words did make me feel better. I can tell that they don't really feel good about another surgery either.

Mom and Dad both put a hand on me, and Mom starts praying, "Father, we bring Tyler to You now and place him before Your throne of grace. Please remove his fear and let him fall asleep quickly and sleep peacefully until tomorrow morning. Put your angels around this bed and touch him with Your love and peace. We love him so much and know You love him even more. In Jesus' name, amen."

I'm glad they prayed I would sleep because that's so hard for me to do the night before surgery. There's a little light from the streetlight outside my window, so I squeeze my eyes tightly shut. I make myself keep my eyes shut and try not to think about the knot in my stomach. I'm sad that I face another surgery. I'm afraid of more pain. I'm even angry that my parents think I need to go through this agony—again.

I must have fallen asleep, because the next time I open my eyes my mom is waking me up. It's still dark outside, and there will be no breakfast for my knotted, and now empty, stomach.

I'm Trapped

I'm buckled in the back seat of the car, soon to be strapped to a torture table. My mom would be terribly upset if she knew I felt so afraid. I try not to show it, but as soon as the hospital doors open before us, I start pulling on my mom's arm, trying to keep her back from them.

"Mom, can't we do this another time?" I beg, as terror fills my little-boy thoughts.

I know where we're headed—to the "holding room" where I'll get ready for surgery. I'm really mad now. This place is so phony . . . all cheerful and fun. A jungle scene is painted really big on the walls, all kinds of video games are on a shelf in one corner, and huge television screens are running kids' shows. I know it's a sham. It's supposed to make little kids feel all happy and forget that they are about to be cut into.

I'm not one of those dumb kids who is tricked into believing this is the way the day will continue. No, I've been here before. I know that sometime soon my "prep" for surgery will begin. And here she comes, the nurse with the dreaded gown in her hand.

"Come on, Tyler," Mom says. "Let's get you changed." But the too-small hospital gown barely covers me. The ties in the back never close all the way, so about a one-inch gap opens all the way down from my neck to my knees. My bare bottom is hanging out for the whole world to see. I'm put in a bed. Playtime is over.

Pretty soon Mom will leave to go change into a sterile gown and cap. I know from experience that she will be back, but the panic starts to bubble up and out of my mouth.

"Mom! Don't go!" I scream.

I don't want her to leave, even for a few minutes. I'm so frustrated at how I feel. I have no power to make anything change. My body won't let me jump up like other kids and try to run out of the room. I'm twisting and turning, feeling helpless while I cry, but I can't get away. *Mom will come back*, I tell myself . . . and she does, but I'm still crying as I'm put on a gurney and wheeled down the hall.

As soon as we enter the surgery theater, that bleach-drenched, super-clean smell hits me in the face. I hate it! I shiver as the cold air wiggles like a snake under the loose end of the sheet lying over me. I wish they'd let me keep my underpants on.

I'm held down and bound to the operating table with sturdy fabric straps. The straps are soft, but I can't move at all.

My arms are stretched out and tied down to bed rods, along with my legs. I squirm and try to twist out of the straps. I think of pictures of Jesus with His arms and legs just like mine, and I don't feel good about this image. I can't protect myself from the beady eyes behind the masks of the doctors and nurses who surround me.

"Let me go! Let me go!" I scream. No one listens.

I'm trapped!

I lie flat on my back on the cold table, terrified. All I can see are two huge lights right above me that blind me. My tears roll down the sides of my face and puddle in my ears so I can't hear well either.

Then I see it! The thing I fear the most! A nurse holds the "sleepy" mask in her hand as she lowers it over my nose and mouth. The sickeningly sweet smell of the gas fills my nostrils and burns my nose. I feel like I can't breathe at all.

"Sweets? Where's Sweets?" I yell through the mask.

I can hear a voice near me say, "Is he actually yelling for candy?"

I'm angry that the doctors and nurses don't know that "Sweets" is what I call my mom.

"Where is my mom?" I scream. "I want my *mom*!"

Just then, one of the bright lights disappears as my mom's face comes into view.

"I'm right here, Tyler. Everything will be okay," she says softly as she takes my hand.

I am, at once, glad but still angry. I'm even angry with myself for being afraid my mom wasn't there. She has promised me over and over again that she will not let them operate on me until she is beside me. I hadn't seen her standing nearby but should have known she was in the room. I'm still angry because she said that everything would be okay. She can't *know* that! I've been with her when doctor after doctor has warned her that any surgery could fail.

In a short while, my thoughts and feelings get fuzzy, and my mom's face starts to blur and fade away from me. I feel her tears falling on my face, mixing with mine.

I know the happy drugs are working cause my body feels so heavy.

Everything slows to a crawl, and then Mom's voice begins to sound like Darth Vader's:

"I-I-I

W-I-I-L-L

B-E-E

H-E-E-E-R-E
W-I-I-I-T-H
Y-O-U-U-U-U-U-U
T-T-Y-Y-L-L-L-E-E-R-R-R-R-R-R-R R R R . . ."

For just a minute, I don't feel afraid.

What seems like seconds later, I feel her tears again. I'm waking up, and her face is close to mine.

"Oh, Tyler, you did so well!" she tells me.

Trusting God and My Parents

That surgery was only one of many, with the same fear tormenting me again and again: more pain, more panic when being strapped down, more uncertainty about the results.

I knew Mom loved me, so I believed her every time she told me: "You have to see the doctor so you can walk better, Tyler."

She was right, but that didn't stop me from protesting or bargaining.

"Oh, Sweet Potato, please, not another one?"

"Why do I need to see *that* doctor again?"

"Sweet Potato, can't we wait just a little while? I'll go later, I promise," I'd plead, even though the passing of time would not relieve the anxiety that preceded every surgery.

When words failed me, my fears, frustrations, and feelings of powerlessness spilled out in sobs and screams. But none of my protests ever succeeded, and before long, Mom and Dad would drive me to another big building where people would do what they could to heal my broken body.

I knew that not only did my parents love me, but God loved me too. I prayed to Jesus and asked Him to heal me like He did for others in the Bible. He did not answer that prayer with instantaneous, miraculous healing.

I still relied on God and Jesus to guide my parents in ways that would follow His plan for my life. I didn't think I would die. I just didn't understand why I had to suffer so much to be able to stand up and walk. I wondered what it would be like to live just one day as a "normal" boy, to hop out of bed in the morning and run downstairs to breakfast before running outside to play with the neighborhood kids on bikes and skateboards. I could not imagine how that freedom of movement would feel. I saw it all around me, but I didn't live it. It was beyond my reach.

I kept praying and believing as God kept leading my parents to put me through more and more surgeries.

Some procedures were short. Some dragged on for hours. And some were downright horrifying. I remember the day one specialist said to my parents, with me still in the room, "Tyler needs this surgery to help him walk, but I have to warn you that if complications develop, he may never walk again."

I freaked out! I squelched a scream because I didn't want to be taken out of the room. I wanted to hear what else the doctor said, but my mind drifted to what "he may never walk again" might mean.

I had progressed enough to walk awkwardly with braces on both legs and help from a walker, but the thought of being forever bound in a wheelchair struck me as a fate much worse than the limited movement I'd finally achieved. I'd been through numerous surgeries and thousands of hours of therapy to get to this point. I didn't want to risk losing what I had accomplished so far.

"I don't know if I can still be me and be happy if I can't walk anymore," I complained, picturing myself falling further and further behind all the "normal" kids at school. "I don't want to disappear and have everyone forget all about me!"

The roller-coaster ride of peering down just before plunging into an abyss and then slowly climbing back up into the arms of Jesus took its toll on me. The knowledge of undergoing another surgery, riding through the emotions until it was over, followed by the recovery—it just exhausted me, as well as my parents.

Even so, that particularly frightening surgery went on as scheduled, as did additional ones. I did finally walk, and I'm still walking today.

My Unusual Normal

Surviving a surgery was always a reason to celebrate. Nurses showered me with toys and all the ice cream I could eat. Family members added to my growing collection of Teenage Mutant Ninja Turtles toys. And I probably played more video games than any other kid my age.

Those perks for suffering through surgery were all terrific, but the joy of them was soon diluted by the everyday life of a child with my limitations.

Any hopes of becoming a "normal" kid like the ones who hang out with friends and lead active, fun-loving lives were soon replaced with hopes that the next surgery or procedure would simply bring me closer to walking better.

I faced new challenges soon after the last dish of ice cream was finished and the last hospital gift was delivered. A painful period of recovery began with countless hours of physical therapy. The therapists pulled and pushed and twisted my body and legs to help me learn to walk independently. I'd sweat and huff and puff and long for each session to be over. It seemed that as soon as I got the hang of new therapies, another surgery was needed. Then, former progress was often stripped away, and I had to start over again.

My parents' attitudes bolstered me through those continuous battles. They never gave up on me, and they never allowed me to give up on myself. Day after day, they provided something more transforming than any procedure: hope.

Whenever nurses, doctors, kids at school, or the world made me focus on all the things I couldn't do, Mom and Dad taught me to dream about everything I would be able to do when my body was better.

"God doesn't make junk, Tyler," they reminded me. "You are a beautiful creation."

The gentle reminder that God doesn't make mistakes, that we are all created in His image, made all the difference to me.

My Physician Friend

While most kids went to school and made friends their own age, I went to medical offices where adults became my friends. My favorite was my pediatrician, Dr. Greg.

He wasn't like the other doctors. He didn't quietly walk from room to room seeing patients. He ran, jumped, and exuded all this wild and crazy energy. He seemed more like a kid himself than like a highly educated professional.

He was also quite the style icon. Colorful shirts adorned with flowers, fish, dogs, and other curious embellishments replaced the plain scrubs most doctors wore. Mismatched socks peeked out from the bottom of his pants. Even his stethoscope was different. When other doctors listened to my heart, their instruments were cold and metallic. But Doctor Greg wrapped his stethoscope in an awesome dinosaur cover.

Not only was he fun loving but also extremely kind. Other doctors came and went, but Dr. Greg was always there for me. He never treated me with condescension or pity. I was just like any other kid to him. I had some medical issues, but otherwise I was a boy with a full life ahead of him. His perpetual smile and positive attitude encouraged me to hang on to whatever dreams of the future I entertained. It didn't matter if my dreams seemed unattainable, Dr. Greg supported me. As much as other doctors told me what I could *not* do, Dr. Greg cheered me on.

I remember one particular day when I entered his office very excited to tell him my latest dream about my future.

"Hey, Tyler, my man," he greeted me. "You look super smiley today. What's up?"

"I know what I want to be when I grow up!" I eagerly said.

"Well, give me the big news." Dr. Greg squatted down and looked at me eye to eye.

"I want to play basketball in the NBA!" I grinned back at him.

"That sounds great, Shaq!" he said with reference to Shaquille O'Neal, the 7'1", 325-pound NBA basketball hero of mine.

"Yeah, I *love* Shaq. He's so good. No one can beat him," I said in a little-boy dreamy voice.

Dr. Greg gave me a high-five and said, "You go for it, Tyler, and I'll help you be just as great as you can possibly be."

He knew that particular dream wouldn't come true, but he saw no reason to destroy my happiness then. He also knew that I would arrive at the same conclusion on my own as I grew up.

And of course as I matured, my dreams did change. I no longer strived to be a professional basketball player. I knew I was destined to be a doctor. My relationship with God deepened to the point that I felt certain He was calling me to help and heal others through professional medicine. The response I often received when sharing this news was that either God or I was mistaken. That's not how Dr. Greg responded. He never once doubted my dream.

When I told him I wanted to attend medical school, he wholeheartedly encouraged me.

Dr. Greg was a healing presence in my life and a barometer of my general well-being. If things were going well, I only saw him once in a while. It's when I *wasn't* doing well that I saw Dr. Greg more often. I enjoyed being with him, but I also knew that it might mean he would need to send me on to one of those *other* doctors. He never sent me to a surgeon unless he knew it was in my best interest. If another surgery was needed, Dr. Greg loved me enough, and was professional enough, to tell me the news I hated to hear.

I knew he was doing the right thing, but I'd become so anxious about the possibility of another surgery that I'd try to avoid him, even if I needed care. I vividly remember friends of mine daring me to ride a skateboard. Now, what would ever possess a handicapped kid with zero balance to get on a skateboard? I'll tell you what would: pride! I was like any young boy who was given a dare—too proud not to at least try it.

I stepped on the skateboard and quickly found myself lying on the ground. So much for pride! I broke a few ribs and dreaded what Dr. Greg would say this time. I tried to think of how I could keep him from finding out about my level of pain. Thankfully, I didn't need to see him for that particular injury, but the incident illustrates how much I wanted to avoid another surgery.

Dr. Greg was not only a healing presence in my life but also a role model for the kind of doctor I dreamed of becoming. I wanted to tell kids that they could go after their dreams despite the naysayers who tried to dampen their aspirations.

With the exception of Dr. Greg, I heard a lot of "No, you can't do that" from a vast number of physicians. But I kept moving forward. I kept looking for ways to become the kind of affirming doctor I wanted to be.

The foundational reason I had hope was my belief and trust in God. I realized that the only way I could become a doctor was by God's grace and intervention in my life. I still don't look like your typical doctor. There were numerous hurdles on the way to becoming a physician that seemed insurmountable, and I didn't soar over them. But I crawled up and over them—and I made it. I'm *Doctor* Tyler now.

I've had a lot of help and support, especially from my parents. They are people of great faith, as you'll see when you read the chapters in this book written by my mom. God used her in so many ways to keep me hanging on to hope when I was dangling from the cliff of despair by my fingernails.

My journey and hers continue in the following chapters, but for now, here's a quick preview.

Reversed Roles

Fast-forward about two decades from the days of my childhood dreams.

I still spend much of my time in the hospital, but there's a big difference. First of all, I'm walking! Second, I'm the doctor taking care of kids who are just as scared as I was all those years ago.

I now walk the long, white hallways where my fear grew with every turn of the gurney wheels as I was taken to surgery for another operation.

I enter rooms where parents try to comfort crying children the way my parents tried to comfort me so many times.

I walk past darkened rooms, respecting the privacy of grieving parents as they absorb bad news.

I don't personally identify with every child or parent here, but I identify with many of them.

And now I do my best to provide medical expertise, comfort, and hope to my patients and their families. I'm the doctor wearing the unusual T-shirts, all of them embellished with superheroes. I say, "Yes," to as many dreams of excited children as I can.

With the unwavering support of individuals like Dr. Greg, my dreams have come true. Today, I'm the chair of pediatrics at Singing River Hospital in the small coastal town of Pascagoula, Mississippi.

I also practice at other hospitals, teach classes on hyperbaric wound healing, run a company and a charitable foundation, write articles for medical journals, serve professional medical organizations and ministries like Focus on the Family, and travel around the world to speak.

Dreams Do Come True

While God has blessed my professional life, He really showed up in my personal life. I prayed frequently and fervently for my future wife. I prayed that God would bless me with someone who would understand what it meant to be married to the handicapped kid. Sure, people thought the little crippled kid with his tiny walker was adorable, but I wondered what they would think when that kid was a full-grown, handicapped man.

In His infinite wisdom and grace, God abundantly answered my prayers for a wonderful family. I met my future wife, Laura, in medical school. We were married in 2012, and together we're raising our beautiful daughter, Harper Grace.

My dreams really have come true.

The story of how that happened is a real testament to God working in my life and in the lives of many other people along the way.

The following chapters will take you along on that journey. You'll read not only my story but my mom's story too: of the ups and downs of raising a child whose limitations could have broken our family apart.

Some of my story may sound a bit familiar to you. The television series *The Good Doctor* based some aspects of the story line on a part of my own life. This television show is about a doctor with autism and savant syndrome who is hired by a prestigious hospital in San Jose, California. I don't have the same disabilities, but the television doctor faces some of the same misunderstandings about his abilities as I have faced with having cerebral palsy.

ABC (American Broadcasting Company) and the television show *20/20* got together to do a segment on *The Good Doctor* by highlighting real-life good doctors. A *20/20* producer read about me and was touched by my journey. As a result, I was featured in the *20/20* episode titled, "The Good Doctors: Brilliance and Bravery." It's a hopeful sign to me that shows like this one may encourage other people struggling with disabilities, or any kind of obstacle in their lives, to fulfill their dreams.

We've titled this book *No Such Thing as Can't* to push back against all the negativity that challenged my dreams and my parents' aspirations for me. My mom kept researching and reading and taking me to doctor after doctor to help me stand up and walk. My dad always, always held on to his God-affirmed belief that I *would* walk one day. Dr. Greg and other faithful friends kept inspiring us when we really wondered if we could remain hopeful that yet another procedure would help me.

We hope you, too, will be inspired to persevere in the pursuit of your own dreams. I've heard that it takes five positive comments to repair the damage from one negative comment. That means we need a lot of positive reinforcement to move through life with all its challenges. We want this book to be a dose of positive reinforcement, and we encourage you to put aside the "you can't" responses that may have come your way. Replace them with "you can!" thoughts that lead you to discover ways to overcome any obstacles you might face. This isn't a candy-coated formula to build you up for a letdown. It's the truth. It takes work and perseverance, but you can achieve far more than you realize when you get out of the "*I can't do this*" mind-set.

While other people may dampen your dreams, there is someone closer who may also bring you down: you! That is certainly understandable when coping with overwhelming feelings of disappointment or discouragement. I understand. There were many times when I held negative self-thoughts too close. You'll see how I overcame those times and kept working to accomplish my own dream.

My mom also faced the danger of negative self-thoughts when she couldn't cope any longer with the pressures of our lives. She reached the deepest depths of depression but is still here to encourage others when they are slipping away from hope. She shares that part of her journey in chapter 7.

This book is honest while being hopeful. It's not always uplifting, but it's real. God is present, as is the reality of doubts and down times. You may not have a child with special needs or be a person with special needs, but you live in this world where all kinds of challenges and victories flavor each day of your life. You have your own dreams . . . some fulfilled and some yet to be fulfilled.

Or perhaps those dreams are gone and have left you with lingering pain. My mom and I hope the vulnerability with which we write our story will at least help bring some healing to any aching places in your heart where sorrow may still live.

If victory is already yours, we hope you'll look at your own life as you read about ours and see where God met you. You may be used by the Lord to help others experience victory also.

No matter where you are in your journey—whether you need to hear this message or pass it along—remember that with God, there's *No Such Thing as Can't*!

2

AN UNEXPECTED KIND OF MOTHERHOOD

"We're putting an IV in your arm now. The caesarean section will be all done when you wake up, and you'll be a new mom," the smiling anesthesiologist calmly whispered to me (Lisa).

The previous three days were a fading blur as I counted backwards . . . ten, nine, eight . . .

Unprepared

January 31, 1985, had started like many other days since Kevin and I had found out we were expecting our first child. Kevin had left for work, and I had gone to my job as an assistant property manager in the apartment building where we lived.

Then, around mid-morning, something strange began happening. I started to wet my pants. I didn't feel like I had to go to the bathroom, but I couldn't stop the intermittent leakage. I wasn't really worried except for the obvious embarrassment that would follow if this leakage continued.

I guess I should call my doctor to see what to do, I thought, still unalarmed.

He told me to come immediately into his office because my water might have broken. I knew to expect my water breaking when the baby was ready to be born, but this wasn't the drenching gushing I'd heard women talk about. And this precious baby boy wasn't due for another 12 weeks.

Now I look back and remember how little knowledge I had about childbirth and anything potentially dangerous that could happen. I didn't know what I didn't know. We didn't have access to instant information like we do now. I couldn't search the internet to better understand what the doctor said. On the other hand, I was spared the troubling "what ifs" that are spelled out on websites today and often cause unnecessary worry and anxiety.

I know it may be hard for a woman today to believe this, but I was still not alarmed. I drove to the doctor's office and just assumed this would be like any other office visit. He'd examine me, determine what to do, and tell me what was next. This was also my first pregnancy, and it had surprised both Kevin and me that our family would be expanding so soon. I was 22 years old and married less than a year. We knew we wanted children, but we intended to wait awhile.

We were excited about this baby, but we were also overwhelmed by the way life was going to change. We were both ill-prepared for a normal pregnancy, much less one that was now showing signs of potential trouble.

My doctor diagnosed me with toxemia and told me to go immediately to the hospital. When I think back, it amazes me how few questions I asked him. I considered him the expert and just did what he told me to do. I think my young age and lack of experience with anything medical contributed to my automatic response to his directions.

The first moments of questioning started to creep into my thinking as I walked into the hospital through the emergency entrance. I still hadn't had the big gush of water breaking, but I knew the intermittent leakage must be more serious than I had thought. I was immediately taken to the maternity wing of the hospital. The nurses were warm and welcoming and talked in comforting ways to ease my now growing concern.

Kevin made it to the hospital shortly after I was settled in the bed in a private room. He hurried over to me, leaned over and kissed me, and said, "What's going on?"

"They're going to induce me," I said in a shaky voice. I didn't know what to expect, and I felt like a little girl going through a big-girl event. Ignorance shielded Kevin and me from knowing what might lie ahead of us, but apprehension was growing. At the same time, we held on to the picture of having a normal baby—early but normal.

The pain and clock watching began as Kevin recorded how far apart my contractions were. My progress was extremely slow. My cervix wasn't dilating, and after two and a half days of labor—yes, two and a half days—the doctor said, "We'll wait six more hours and then do a C-section."

We were quickly running out of time for a normal delivery. The monitors on my stomach indicated that Tyler was in distress. My water was still leaking, and I wasn't progressing any further. My emotions finally caught up with reality—my love for my baby was immeasurable! Tyler and I were in a battle for his very life. I longed to have him outside of my body and in my arms. The words "in distress" really scared me. I had no idea exactly what those words meant or what a baby in distress would look like. It was the first time I went from thinking we were having a baby who might be little and need oxygen to a baby who might really have serious health issues.

I was wheeled into an operating room and the anesthesiologist spoke to me.

Our Baby Has Problems

I opened my eyes to the sight of Kevin sitting next to my bed with his head in his hands. The grogginess I'd had in the recovery room was still heavy, but I could see that Tyler was not in the room with us.

Ever since we found out we were pregnant, I'd held an image in my mind of holding my newborn baby in my arms. He'd be swaddled in a warm blanket and curling his tiny fingers around one of my fingers as he first felt my love skin-to-skin.

"Kevin!" I said in a weak but urgent voice. "Where's Tyler?"

Kevin stood up and sat on the side of the bed. "I've seen him, Lisa. It's bad. He may not make it," he said in the trembling voice of a man whose soul was scorched with pain. Tears spilled down his grief-stricken face.

I was crying, unable to even say anything when Kevin spoke again, "He has toxemia. I can't hold him, and you can't hold him. They're taking him to a neonatal unit . . ."

"Mr. and Mrs. Sexton," a voice interrupted Kevin.

Two people dressed in flight medical suits were wheeling an incubator into the room. They told me they were transferring Tyler by helicopter to Lee Memorial Hospital in Ft. Myers, four hours by car from our home in Bradenton, Florida.

I could barely grasp what they were telling me. I wanted to see my son. I wanted them to bring the incubator closer so I could see him! My mind was racing.

What do they mean that I can't hold him? I have to hold him!

I was no longer groggy. I was determined!

"Please sign these papers," one of the flight personnel said to me.

"Sorry to bother you, but this permission has to be signed by the mother. No one else can do this."

I scrawled my signature on the bottom line and pushed the paper aside.

They stepped back as they wheeled the incubator next to the bed.

"You can touch his hand," a nurse said as she pointed to the hole in the side of the incubator.

I looked at him, with tubes coming out all over his body, and I no longer demanded to hold him. I touched his tiny fingers, fully understanding that we had a perilous journey ahead of us. Tyler was all puffed up and looked like he would pop if a pin stuck him. My heart swelled with love for him.

One of the flight personnel was telling me that his lungs could collapse when they reached a certain altitude.

"I didn't know how much I loved him until I saw him," I sobbed to the female flight medical person. "Please take care of him."

She took my hand and gently said, "I'm a mother, and I'm very good at what I do. I will take care of your little boy."

They quickly wheeled Tyler away to the waiting helicopter.

Kevin and I clung to each other and cried uncontrollably.

"You have to go, Kevin. You need to be with our boy," I said as I pulled back from him.

"I hate to leave you."

I encouraged Kevin to go even though I couldn't. I'd just had surgery and still had toxemia. It was awful to see him leave, but it was a relief to think that he'd make the four-hour drive to Ft. Myers and get to be with Tyler.

Later that day, I received a call in my hospital room from the doctor in Ft. Myers. He told me that Kevin had arrived. Then he gave me the bad news: Soon after taking off, the higher altitude caused Tyler's lung to collapse. A chest tube was inserted to stabilize him, but then later in the flight the other lung collapsed. Another tube helped him hang on until they got him to the hospital.

"I know you can't leave to come here yet, but your son's condition is hour by hour," the doctor spoke solemnly into the phone. "If he doesn't make it, we'll keep him on a respirator so his body will be warm when you hold him and love on him before you have to bury him."

I felt like I couldn't breathe. No words can explain the horror of those words or the agony of waiting to go to Tyler.

Four days later, I was released from the hospital. Kevin drove back from Ft. Myers to pick me up. My doctor told me I had to go home and rest an additional number of days before going to Ft. Myers. I got in the car, looked at Kevin, and said, "You know we aren't going home, don't you?"

A New Journey Begins

On the drive to Ft. Myers, Kevin told me that Tyler had tubes coming out of every part of his little body and a tube to help him breathe.

We didn't really talk after that. The reality of our baby boy's condition gripped our hearts with the frightening possibility that he might not even survive.

As a precaution after my C-section, I was taken up to the neonatal floor by wheelchair. The nursery we walked into revealed the intensive care these infants needed. Incubators were lined up with multiple monitors around each bed. The nurse who greeted us explained that any touch could bring up Tyler's heart rate. We could lightly and briefly touch his foot, but that was all he could tolerate. His head had been shaved, and he was still puffed up as a result of the toxemia.

"He knows his mommy's voice," the nurse softly told me. "You can talk to him."

I leaned over to talk to him, and a tear fell gently on his shoulder. Many years and many surgeries later, Tyler told me that when he came out of anesthesia after all those surgeries, he could feel my tears on his face. He knew his mommy would always be there.

Sacred Ground

Kevin needed to return to work after spending a number of days with Tyler in the hospital. He commuted back and forth between work in Bradenton and Ft. Myers. We stayed in frequent contact during all the 95 days of Tyler's stay.

A small room with a private bathroom in the hospital became my home for those 95 days, and the neonatal unit became the sacred ground of precious infants struggling to stay alive. My routine was the same every day: get up and dressed; go sit by Tyler's bed in the rocking chair that graced the side of the incubator; visit with the other parents; leave very briefly to grab something to eat; and go to bed with prayers for Tyler and all the other little ones on my lips as I fell asleep.

Day after day of being in the neonatal unit was like living in an aquarium. You're swimming around the babies you can't touch, falling in love with this mom or that mom, talking to the anxious dads who are there as much as their work allows, following the progress of all the tiny ones hanging on to life, and adapting to the small world in that enclosed space. You have no privacy, but those other inhabitants become your people. Bonds are woven unlike many others you will ever experience. You celebrate with them when they say good-bye to you with their healing infant in their arms, and you welcome the next one who arrives in tears as their baby is wheeled in.

And when waiting doesn't end with a baby going home, you grieve with the devastated parents. Kevin and I watched women weep with unbearable grief and grown men fall on their knees next to the incubator of their struggling baby who struggled no more. We couldn't help but silently wonder if that would be us in the next hour, the next day, the next week. We asked ourselves, *When would it happen?* And we asked God, *Why would Tyler survive when these other innocent little ones did not? Would Tyler survive?*

I began to bargain with God. *Will You heal him, God, please, if I volunteer more or give more money to the church, or confess any possible sin I have committed or am committing now?* I knew we were no different from the parents crumbled with grief before us, so why wouldn't we lose our baby too? Why were they losing theirs?

I'd heard people say, "God won't give you more than you can handle," but that's a lie. I had more than I could handle. Some of those parents lying on the floor and clinging to each other were only alive because they were breathing. They were dying in all other ways. They couldn't handle their loss.

In those moments, I didn't understand why a God of love would let this happen. I started to read familiar Scripture verses of comfort and promises of hope.

Philippians 4:13 (NASB) says, "I can do all things through Him who strengthens me." The words "through Him" jumped off the page and into my heart. And then I read Proverbs 3:5: "Trust in the LORD with all your heart, and do not lean on your own understanding." Trusting doesn't require human understanding. I let that need go.

In my little room near the neonatal unit, I fell down at the feet of Jesus and cried out to Him. *I can't handle this without You, Jesus. I don't understand why some children die and others do not. But I trust You. I believe You have a plan for my life and for the lives of the families in that aquarium with me. No matter what happens, You are sovereign. Help me. Please!*

I had more than I could handle, and that's when I knew how very much I needed God. Only "with Him" could I live through this pain.

We can trust God when we live with Jesus Christ as our Lord and Savior. What I learned during the three months in that sealed environment allowed me to be able to move through what was to come. No matter what would happen, I could still trust and praise God.

The fact that God helped me survive wasn't because I was any better than any of those parents who lost their children. God's love and grace wasn't something I could earn by bargaining with God. I didn't deserve it. It was, and is, a gift to me if I accepted it. Jesus continues to help me and my family live through difficulties we never knew we'd face.

What about those other parents who lost children? I don't know their stories after we left the neonatal unit. But God does. He loves them. And I trust Him with them.

God's plan for our lives took an exciting turn 95 days after that life-saving helicopter ride.

We're Going Home

Little by little, Tyler grew stronger over the next three months. We got excited over any tiny victory on the road toward going home.

A milestone for Kevin and me was the day we were finally able to hold Tyler for the first time. The nurse brought him in and gave us instructions on how to gently accomplish this maneuver without squeezing him. He had to lie flat—first on my lap and then on Kevin's so he didn't receive too much stimulation. After a very short three minutes of holding time, the nurse took Tyler from our first embrace and back to the neonatal unit.

Kevin is not usually a crier. He's a strapping 6'4" of "all guy." But he cried the first time he saw Tyler, and he cried that day we first held our baby boy. We sobbed and sobbed, with relief and the first glimmer of hope that we might really be able to take Tyler home.

Every day of those three months in the hospital I'd ask the

doctor if we could take Tyler home. One day I decided not to bother him anymore. Unbeknownst to me, on that day the doctor was actually *waiting* for me to ask the question!

"Don't you have something to ask me?" the smiling doctor said.

And before I could answer, he said, "Well, today is the day."

It was our celebration day with the nurses, doctors, and the other parents we loved so much. They were truly happy for us. We left with hugs, kisses, well-wishes, and Tyler swaddled in our arms.

Dashed Dreams

A little snippet of doubt began to creep into our joy as the months passed by. Tyler was doing great except he seemed to be slow in achieving developmental milestones. His pediatrician assured me it was normal for him to be behind the curve on some things because he was born prematurely. Because of that, I'd read about what to expect at a certain age and then add three months to Tyler's age. If a baby should start to sit up independently between four and seven months, I'd expect Tyler to do that around seven to ten months. At a year old he would sit up and quickly fall over. Other milestones came and went, and Tyler didn't hit them. Finally, at 18 months, his pediatrician referred him to a neurologist.

I wasn't worried about brain damage even though we were going to see a neurologist. Tyler was so verbal and smart. He loved to chatter away, and his vocabulary was well developed for his age. I couldn't imagine anything being wrong with his brain. It was physical limitations that hampered him.

That initial visit resulted in an MRI and then a return visit to the neurologist for the results. We met with the doctor and his nurse in his office. Anxiety hit me when the nurse closed the door. After a bit of small talk, the doctor got straight to the point.

"Your son has brain damage," the doctor said in a conciliatory voice.

"He can't," I said. "He's so smart!"

"Tyler's problems are not with his brain's mental ability," he quietly said. "It's with his muscles. He has cerebral palsy. He may never walk. His body is very tight, so he'll need surgery and intense physical therapy."

He went on to explain other things that would later become comprehensible. At that moment, I couldn't get my head around it. I just kept thinking, *But he's so smart! He's so smart! How can he have brain damage?*

As we left the doctor's office, the nurse gave me several pamphlets about cerebral palsy. She was telling me that they would explain what to do next and how to get started with specialists and treatment plans.

I waited for Kevin to get home that night to tell him the results of the MRI. He was playing with Tyler on the floor, and I sat down with them. As I uttered the words "cerebral palsy," Kevin's eyes revealed the shock we both felt. We looked through the pamphlets from the doctor's office and tried to grasp what this all meant.

We grieved the loss of our boy growing up to be a basketball player like Kevin. He had played in high school and still played with other adult men in local leagues. He loved all sports and deeply felt the loss of teaching his son the things he loved. We stood at the door of Tyler's room after putting him to bed and shed tears at the sight of all the sports décor that surrounded our sleeping baby—the curtains, wallpaper, pictures, Tyler's clothes hanging in the closet—all of them covered with basketballs, footballs, baseballs, and all manner of sports gear.

The next morning I shut the windows, closed the blinds, and sealed us off from the outside world. Kevin and I mourned for three days. We still trusted God and believed He would sustain us, but at the same time, we faced our loss. We cried and prayed and hurt. God met us. He didn't "fix" Tyler, but His love held us. On the fourth day, Kevin went back to work, and I opened our home back up to the Florida sun.

I was ready to begin this new adventure of ours and figure it out. We'd made it through 95 days of complications after Tyler's birth, and we'd get through this too! *We will fix this*, I thought. I was ready to understand more.

Pretty soon I would be praising God for His grace that sunny morning. My ignorance as to what was ahead of us was a gift.

I'm still praising God for the love and continued grace He provided as those struggles and challenges unfolded over time.

3

CHALLENGES OF THE EARLY YEARS

"Give me Emi! Give me Emi," Tyler said with his arms flapping in excitement. I (Lisa) had just gotten him out of the car and into his wheelchair. He was ready to hug his six-month-old baby sister, Emilee, and help me get the three of us into the physical therapy facility.

I placed Emi in Tyler's lap, facing him with her little legs on either side of his body, and fastened his seat belt around both of them. His legs may have been unable to function, but his arms wrapped lovingly around his baby sister, holding her securely.

Diaper bag over one shoulder, purse over the other, and hands on the wheelchair handles, I pushed Tyler and Emi toward the facility door to evaluate yet another physical therapist. We'd been through this routine several times before and failed to meet the perfect person to work with Tyler.

Would this therapist be different? Would she relate well to Tyler? Would she be compassionate but firm? Would she treat him with kindness and me with patience? Would she be an encourager or a threatening force?

We would soon find out!

A Guiding Star

We walked and wheeled into a beehive of activity. Children, adult patients, and therapists were busy working with the equipment strategically placed all over this room. There were therapy beds with mats on them and straps and pulleys hanging down from other devices designed for all kinds of physical therapy. While it was a bit overwhelming, it was also bright and inviting.

I walked up to one of the therapists, who turned around just as I approached. Her smile beamed a welcome and, after greeting me, she immediately knelt down and said to Tyler, "Hi! I'm Michelle." He grinned back at her, and I thought we might have found the right person to work with Tyler.

Michelle walked us over to one of the therapy beds, explaining to Tyler that she was going to look at his legs and see what exercises she could help him with. He didn't really understand much, but he liked this sweet woman with the kind voice.

Emilee was asleep in my arms, so Michelle took Tyler out of his wheelchair and put him on one of the beds. He willingly let her take off his braces and move his legs. Tyler was a little over three years old and had been examined many times over his short life. I could tell by the look on his face that he trusted Michelle. She spoke softly and positively to him as she moved his little legs and feet to determine their tightness.

After her evaluation, Michelle looked me in the eye.

"I'm going to be honest, Lisa," she said. "You need to know that your son will always have physical limitations. But here's the good news: I'm going to help Tyler be the very best Tyler he can be, but I'll need you to be committed for the long haul—it will be a long journey to get him there, and it will be tough. But we can do it." I had an immediate peace about her. It takes a special person to be positive and honest at the same time when dealing with a parent and child who have heard lots of bad news. Not only did she relate beautifully to Tyler, but she was kind, yet firm, with me. I just loved her to pieces. Over the years, she and her family became lifelong friends. Her son, Brian, used to babysit for Tyler and Emilee. Tyler thought Brian was so much fun! One of his favorite playtimes with Brian was when he would take Ty's socks off and pull him around on the hardwood floors, something any little boy would love.

We saw Michelle several times a week and more often after surgeries. When therapy was particularly painful, Ty would say, "I don't like you today, 'Chell."

She would respond with: "I don't like your attitude today, but I still love you."

He would relax enough for her to finish his workouts and then be rewarded with a piece of Juicy Fruit gum and a sticker. They understood each other, and even when he cried, he trusted her.

God sent an angel to us in the person of Michelle Larson. I could never repay her for her kindness and expertise that impacted our lives so positively. She helped me understand decisions that needed to be made with doctors, surgeons, and treatments, as well as what Kevin and I had to do with Tyler at home. Michelle was so much more than Tyler's physical therapist: she touched my heart with a healing therapy in those early years that made a huge difference in my life. Our challenging journey was moving forward, and God had sent me a loving, guiding star.

The Surgery Roller Coaster

Tyler underwent 17 surgeries by the time he was in middle school.

That first day of any surgery was especially challenging for Kevin and me. It placed us back in the position of feeling helpless. We knew we'd made the best possible decision for our boy, but surgery would put him through so much additional pain. He was too young to understand what was happening, but we knew that the future held untold obstacles he'd need to overcome. Nurses would give us gowns and masks to put on and let us walk on either side of his gurney as he was wheeled to the operating room. They would let me go into the operating room with him to relieve some of his stress, but we went right back to the surgery waiting room as soon as he was under the anesthesia.

Kevin and I sat in that waiting room with other terrified parents, hoping, praying, and trying to cope with hours of terror. After a seeming eternity, our surgeon would come out and give us the results. The relief that Tyler was okay washed over us as we prepared for the details of what would come next.

Tyler then faced rehab therapy for days, weeks, or months, only to be faced with another surgery to get him one step closer to walking.

No Play Dates

Mornings often started with the sound of Tyler combat crawling (scooting along on his belly since he couldn't get his legs up to crawl on all fours) along the hallway. He woke up with a smile and was ready for another day!

Every morning I'd kiss his little legs as I followed Michelle's instructions on how to successfully put on his braces. I was worried about doing this task the right way, along with every other detail of Tyler's care. Michelle sat me down and gently but adamantly told me that she was the therapist, and I was the mom. I was wearing myself out thinking I had to do everything for Tyler.

"When you're at home," she said, "you don't have to do therapy. Do life!"

So we came home and did life! Breakfast, go to therapy, come home and play on the floor, lunch, naptime, playtime, dinner, bath, bed. Life!

The main difference for us was we didn't go on play dates with other moms and kids. Some of my friends whose kids understood about Tyler invited us, but I wanted to protect him from noticing his obvious physical limitations compared to the other kids. In reality, I was really protecting myself.

I knew what the routine for the other moms and kids would be, and we couldn't be part of that. I could just imagine the conversations between the other moms.

"Tommy went for his swimming lesson the other day."

"Bobby just started soccer. It's so cute to see all these little guys running around."

"Well, we had a bad day. Billy missed a party to the zoo because he had a summer cold."

"Oh, I know. Doctor visits just break into my whole day!"

"Susie fell the other day, and her little cut got infected!"

"We just got the school schedule for fall, and Nancy didn't get the teacher we wanted. I'm so frustrated."

What would I say? "Tyler and I went to PT and scheduled his next surgery. Then he'll need to be fitted for new braces." And then I'd have to run and pick him up with his braces full of mulch from crawling and start the whole process of loading us back into the car. I had a real pity party going on in my mind.

As I repeatedly ruminated on how a play date would unfold, one particular image always broke my heart: After getting Emilee and Tyler up and dressed and fed and loaded into the car, we'd head to the park. We'd pull into the parking lot, Tyler in his booster seat looking with eager expectation for what was to come. Car doors would open and kids would come spilling out all around us. Little boys and girls would run squealing toward the swings and slides as their moms shouted meaningless words of caution to slow down. The moms would head to the benches to sit and chat and drink the coffees they had stopped to get on their way to the park. Tyler, Emilee, and I would just be starting our slow trip from the car to the swings. Tyler would never be jumping out of a car and joining all the other kids who ran on strong, fast legs.

No, we would play at home.

I wasn't mad or angry with those moms and kids. I just didn't want to be around them and what we would never have.

I wish I'd given Tyler more opportunities to try and fail, try and adjust, try and succeed, but I wasn't at that point yet.

Leaving the Bubble

Michelle encouraged us to put Tyler into preschool when he turned four. She could see my hesitancy, but she talked me through the reality that he was ready for socialization that was so needed for him to experience a full life. He was using a walker by that time and excited about this new adventure.

He adjusted well to preschool and was ready to move ahead from a few hours several days a week to full-time, "regular" school, but was I? I know all moms go through this process of letting go of their precious little ones, and I'm no different. But it was still hard. I had to recognize this challenge as an opportunity for Tyler to experience success.

Big Boy School

I was a nervous wreck. The first day of big boy school had arrived! Tyler was happy and chattering away. He was so smart and engaging and really a happy, friendly little boy.

Would the kids accept those wonderful qualities in spite of his braces and walker, his awkwardness on the playground, and his need for extra help to get around?

He wore new duds for this special day: bright red shorts, a sparkling white T-shirt tucked neatly into his shorts, and brand-new white Reebok tennis shoes. I knew how the drop-off routine worked and realized it prevented me from going into the school with him. Driving to school, I could see Tyler in my rearview mirror, just beaming away. We took our place in the carpool line and inched along toward the drop-off point.

My hands were sweaty, and I held back tears, determined to show Tyler that I was excited for him. Our turn to unload came. I hopped out of the car and put his walker by his door. I scooped him up and into his walker. He took off in the direction of the other children after waving to me and saying, "I'll see you soon, Mama!"

I pulled away and cried and cried. Emilee and I went to the store and were back at the school at 11:15 a.m. for his noon pickup. Time ticked slowly by, and finally a bell rang and the doors of the school swung open with eager groups of kids running out to be picked up. Tyler was in the middle of them, smiling and scooting along in his walker. The school attendant at the curb opened my van door, and Tyler said, "Oh, Mama, I'm so sorry! I got filthy dirty today." His apology was accompanied by the biggest smile! I just hugged him and got him in his booster seat.

When we got home, I took his braces and shoes off and sand poured out of his shoes. "I went in the sandbox! It was so much fun. The kids were really nice . . ." He just wouldn't stop talking. He told me about a boy named Kevin McCann who became his friend. The teacher had asked the children what they wanted to be when they grew up. Tyler said, "I want to be a basketball player." When it came to Kevin's turn, he said, "I want to be Tyler's legs when I grow up so he can be what he wants to be."

I learned a lesson that day. Other people could teach Tyler things that I couldn't teach him. Kevin taught him that other children could unselfishly love him. His teachers taught him that they believed in him enough to let him figure out how to play on the playground with braces on. He learned on his own that he loved being out enjoying new experiences.

Bert Is Still Bert

When the long-running television show *Sesame Street* first aired in 1969, an engaging host of Muppets characters entered the homes of almost every family with young children. Big Bird, Bert and Ernie, Cookie Monster, Oscar the Grouch, the Count, and others launched a commercial enterprise that has lasted for more than 50 years.

By the time Tyler started school and Emilee was a curious toddler, small toy images of these characters had become an important part of Tyler's life. He had collected masses of them, partly because they were gifts from his many visitors during his hospital stays. People would ask me what they could bring to him. These toys were sold everywhere from checkout racks in grocery stores to fancy stores, and later online. They were inexpensive and thoughtful gifts that Tyler loved. They added some fun times to long hours in a hospital bed.

When the *Sesame Street* gang wasn't at the hospital with Tyler, they lived on the fireplace hearth in our living room. He would line them up on the hearth when he and Emilee weren't playing with them and easily take them off the hearth at playtime.

One afternoon after lunch, Tyler asked me a question that he had never directly asked before: "Mama, why aren't my legs like the other kids' legs at school?" I was surprised and needed a little time to think about my answer, so I told him we'd talk about it after his nap. I had known that someday he would ask this question, and I'd be faced with the challenge of sensitively answering it. I certainly didn't know it would be in the way that it happened.

Back in the kitchen, cutting up vegetables for dinner and thinking about what to say to Tyler, my eyes fell on the *Sesame Street* gang on the living room hearth. I walked over and picked up Bert. Without a lot of thought but with a fair amount of determination, I went back to the kitchen and cut off Bert's arms with the butcher knife! I threw his severed arms in the trash can, and put Bert back in his place on the hearth.

A little later I could hear Tyler combat crawling down the hallway from his bedroom. He went right over to the hearth and said, "Oh my word! What happened to Bert's arms?"

I sat down on the hearth with him and said, "Bert was in a car accident and had to have his arms amputated. People in the world will call him unkind names, and he won't be able to do all the things that everybody else does."

"Like me and my legs," Tyler said as he looked up at me.

"That's right, Tyler."

I went on to tell him that he had something called cerebral palsy. We talked about what that meant and how Tyler, like Bert, would learn what he could do and what he could not do. He would also learn to do lots of things other people do, but in different ways.

As he held Bert and looked at him, I said, "You see, Bert is still Bert. And you are still Tyler."

He said, "All right, I understand."

He didn't ask a lot of questions. He didn't cry. It was as if he really did understand and accepted the truth of his condition. He held on to Bert and smiled at him. When Emilee got up, Tyler sat with her and told her exactly what I had told him. That's when I knew for sure he really did understand.

Eggs in a Basket

As I watched Tyler lovingly hold the armless Bert, I remembered my most significant lesson in learning to trust God with my son's life.

It happened at the time Tyler was in preschool and mastering how to use a walker. When he would let go of the walker, he would simply fall on his knees. Then he would crawl around on all fours because his legs were finally able to push his bottom up in the air.

He couldn't squat yet, but Michelle assured me he was close to being able to hold on to his walker, bend down to pick something up, and stand upright again. She was preparing me to let that "something" be Easter eggs!

Our city was going to have a huge Easter egg hunt, and Michelle believed she would have Tyler ready to hang on to his walker, stop and squat, pick up eggs, stand up, drop them in his basket, and go get more eggs. She thought it would be a good experience for him and that he'd love it. I wasn't so sure, but I agreed to let him try.

She first mentioned this idea in the fall, so she had about six months to work with him. They set goals and worked hard at physical therapy, water therapy, horse therapy . . . all building up to being at the starting line with hundreds of other kids on Easter weekend.

Tyler loved goals, and he loved the Juicy Fruit gum reward for the hours of hard work he had to do to be ready. Sure enough, as Easter time rolled around, he could successfully complete the whole process. It was more of a marathon than a sprint. He didn't do anything in a hurry, and he couldn't run, so going from one egg to another would take him a long time.

Little Emilee was entering the race too. Uncharacteristically, I splurged and went to the most expensive stores in town to buy matching outfits for this excited duo. Emilee wore a pink dress with smocking and matching pink bloomers with her name embroidered across the back of them. She had ruffled socks and white shoes and her shining brown curls bounced when she walked. Tyler's white shorts and pink polo shirt matched his sister's outfit, and his new white tennis shoes and white socks finished off his look!

As we drove up to the field where the race was being held, reality hit me right in the face—it was so crowded. I began to think that I had made a big mistake to let Michelle talk me into this all those months ago. But it was too late to turn back now. Tyler and Emilee were undaunted. They couldn't wait to get out of the car and over to the starting line.

Suddenly they were there, standing with literally hundreds of other kids, and Tyler hanging on to his walker. The starting gun went off and a huge burst of kids took off. Tyler was left there with Emilee standing next to him, and I was furious. What had I done? I had made major strides with him to get him out into the world, and now I'd be the mom who put him in this place. He'd have no eggs! My sunglasses hid the tears welling up in my eyes as I turned away from the sight in front of me. It took me several minutes to get myself together and turn back to Tyler and Emilee.

They weren't there on the starting line! I looked down the field and could see them among other children. I headed toward them to scoop them into my arms and tell them I was sorry. As I got closer, Tyler saw me and shouted, "Look at all the eggs in my basket!" His basket was full, and he'd put some in Emilee's basket too.

"All the kids were running so fast that their eggs were popping out of their baskets, so I just picked them up," he said with the biggest grin on his face. He was thrilled!

Trusting God

I went down on my knees, sobbing. Two Easter baskets full of eggs split my heart wide open so I could hear my Father say, "I need you to give this little boy to Me. His basket may not always be full, and he won't be first in everything he tries to do, but he will be blessed beyond measure. I need you to trust Me."

I gave Tyler and Emilee to the Lord that day. I looked at those eggs in the two baskets and saw them symbolizing the blessings that were to come. I could feel the Holy Spirit touching my spirit in a way I had not known before. Words are inadequate to explain moments with God that transcend our circumstances. Those moments touch us in the deep crevices of our souls where only God Himself can reach.

I wish I could tell you that I was totally transformed from that day on. But life doesn't seem to happen that way. I woke up the next morning the same Lisa—a worrywart, a crybaby, a person who was protective and nervous about the future. No, I wasn't totally transformed, but I was changed: I saw that I could not determine the outcome of every situation that Tyler would face; I realized I needed to face the challenges he would encounter without defining success in the way the world defines it; and I accepted, with amazement, that God works in ways I could never anticipate. I knew a lot about me would not quickly change, but I was confident God could change my thinking as I got to know Him better.

I intentionally decided to make a daily choice to pray and to pray *big*! I began to really believe how incredibly awesome and incomprehensible God is.

In the midst of times when worries and fears crept back into my thinking, I could imagine Jesus wrapping His arms around me and saying, *Oh sweet, darling daughter of Mine, you have no idea what I can do and what I have in store for this boy and this girl. Just trust Me.*

I understood that I had a choice to make. Experiencing the love of God in my life meant I needed to know Him more deeply. I committed to read the Scriptures, claim the promises, and learn about Christ. To totally trust Him, I must know Him. That process, like Tyler's process of learning to squat and pick up Easter eggs, takes time. It's a marathon, not a sprint.

I claimed the prayer for myself that Paul prayed for the Philippians:

> And it is my prayer that your love may abound more and more, with knowledge and all discernment, so that you may approve what is excellent, and so be pure and blameless for the day of Christ, filled with the fruit of righteousness that comes through Jesus Christ, to the glory and praise of God.
>
> PHILIPPIANS 1:9-11

Challenges arrive in all shapes and forms, and the more I know Jesus, the more my love and discernment will grow. My deep desire is to know God and trust Him completely.

4

GOD MADE ME TO BE ME

It was the first day of fourth grade and time to go to physical education class. I (Tyler) knew what to expect, and I was not excited: kids running around; curious stares coming in my direction; choosing teams with me being the last one picked; everyone laughing at my awkward movements and physical pain while trying to do what the other kids were doing.

"Hi, Tyler," Mr. Pike greeted me. "Do you want to shoot some hoops to get warmed up?" he asked as if I was just like all the other kids. I thought he was talking to someone behind me, so I didn't even answer his question.

He didn't make a big deal about what I would do during the beginning of this first PE class. It was as if he didn't notice that my body was twisted and my gait abnormal. I was used to being the odd man out in this setting and didn't quite know what to make of this warm and engaging teacher.

On that first day of PE—a class that was always tough for me—Mr. Pike set the stage for the other kids to see how to treat me. I felt special receiving his validation of me as a part of the group of students and not singled out as the disabled kid. There would be lots of times when those things I dreaded happened, but Mr. Pike always had my back. He was a fun-loving and kind man who made this PE class a blast, even for me.

After that first day, he would start each class by filling the air with his famous "Pike Howl," a low, guttural growl that grew louder and louder. That howl meant *let's have some fun!* We would yell back *yyyyeeeeaaaahhhh!* And off we'd go with the enthusiasm of kids released from the confinement of desks and walls. I ran slower and moved awkwardly, but I tried everything everyone else did. I knew that Mr. Pike had asked my mom what my limitations were, and she'd said, "He can do anything he wants to do. He may not do it as well or it may take him longer, but he'll give it his all."

Meeting a Goal

Our school participated in the President's Fitness Challenge in which students would have to do 50 sit-ups and 50 push-ups and then run a mile. I remember that day well as we all headed to the track for the mile run. Mr. Pike told me I didn't have to participate, but I really wanted to give it a try. I'd heard about the four-minute mile, a seemingly impossible time that was achieved in 1954 by a guy named Roger Bannister. Naysayers in the running world said it could not be done: No one could run a mile in under four minutes. Before he ran the mile in 3.59.4, Bannister must have determined to go for a goal of proving the skeptics wrong.

That day as I stood on the starting line of the school track, I knew my own goal was no four-minute mile. I also knew that no one watching me anticipated that I could even make it around the track four times. It seemed impossible for a kid with cerebral palsy (CP) to manage to go that distance, regardless of how long it might take. I wanted to prove them wrong. My goal was to finish the race.

We were lined up, ready to go when the starting gun blasted off. Adrenalin was pumping through my veins as I began the first of the four laps. *This is okay*, I thought. I can do this. *Just keep moving.* I was not surprised when all the other kids bolted ahead of me. I knew I would be last during the whole race but kept my mind on my goal of finishing.

Pretty soon I realized that runners were lapping me, passing me before I had finished that first lap. As I headed into my second lap my body was screaming. Every part of me agonized in pain. But at least I was upright and moving.

Mr. Pike walked some of the way next to me, encouraging me with kind words and smiles. Another one of the kids came out and walked with me during another lap. After the very slowest runner passed the finish line, I was alone on the track.

As I rounded the last curve in the track for the fourth time, I could see the finish line. If I could make it to that mark etched into the track surface, I would have achieved my goal. One aching step at a time. One gasping breath at a time. For a moment everything around me blurred, and all I could see was the lane in front of me that led to my goal: the finish line!

My vision expanded again, and I saw a group of the runners cheering me on from the finish line and the crowds in the stands doing the same thing. *Go Tyler! You've got this! You can do it!* Mixed emotions filled my mind: joy and excitement that I would reach my goal and sadness that everyone had to wait for me. Feeling overwhelmed, I silently called out to God for help. *Please keep my legs moving! Please give me another breath to make it!* I saw the hurdles next to the track that athletes could actually soar over, and here I was struggling to keep walking. My hurdles were as huge to me as those physical hurdles must have been to the runners who leaped over them.

God answered my prayer. I crossed the finish line to the hugs and applause of the kids on the track and the fans in the stands. It was a moment to remember. And I'm forever grateful to Mr. Pike. He never made me feel unusual or out of place. He knew I gave my all to whatever we did in class, and he allowed me the opportunity to compete in an event just like the other kids, even if it took me longer. I might have looked awkward, but I finished the mile run!

Worst Day

I remember only one day in all of elementary school when Mr. Pike wasn't there. We were gathering for PE on the outdoor basketball court when a substitute teacher appeared. He was shorter than Mr. Pike and walked with a bit of a swagger that silently said he was the boss for the day. He stood with his hands on his hips and wore a baseball cap on his balding head. A shiny whistle hung around his neck from a thick cord.

We were lined up and doing jumping jacks like we always did at the beginning of class. I was next to my best friend Bobby and doing the best I could. If I concentrated and coordinated all my muscles, I could lift myself off the asphalt by about half an inch, as kids around me seemed to be jumping sky-high. I compensated by strenuously waving my arms above my head.

The next thing we knew, the substitute teacher blew his whistle in an ear-splitting blast that snapped us all into attention. He pointed right at me and yelled, "Quit clowning around, kid! You're in the fourth grade! Is that the best jumping jack you can do?"

I turned beet red with embarrassment. Everyone was looking at me. The big, noisy throng of kids suddenly turned strangely silent. Then gales of laughter interrupted the silence. I just stood there, feeling all broken up inside. My throat tightened to keep me from screaming out or crying. Bobby put a hand on my shoulder, and some other kids who hadn't laughed sent sympathetic looks my way.

The teacher resumed barking out orders as I walked over to the edge of the court. I sat down and put my head in my hands. I didn't want to make eye contact with anyone, especially the teacher. No way would I stand back up again and risk being pointed out for my imperfections. I couldn't handle any more derisive laughter or humiliation.

The rest of the day was a blur. I went to my classes but didn't participate at all. When a question about a lesson was asked I didn't shoot my hand up to answer. I didn't chat with Bobby who was trying to get me out of my slump. My mind kept rerunning the mental video of the moment when the PE class was shaken by the shrill sound of that whistle. The image of the teacher's face and pointed finger haunted me as I continually relived my humiliation.

When Mom picked me up, I was pretty quiet. We usually talked about every little detail that had happened that day, from my account of when a kind word made me feel good to Mom's report of a broken nail. That day I couldn't muster any small talk.

Finally, I told her, "I don't want to be me anymore." She had a dramatic response to that statement.

God's Design

As soon as we got home, Mom went into action. She headed straight for my room and began grabbing all my stuff. She threw some shoes and clothes out into the hallway and carried some of the breakable items—lamps, a stereo, a radio alarm clock—out to the living room. She didn't say anything, but she moved with steely determination.

I watched this procession with confusion and a growing anger. *What the heck is she doing now?* I wondered. When you're a kid, there's little that you can call your own. But here was my mom, invading my private sanctum and taking all my worldly possessions.

In a matter of moments, toys, puzzles, sawhorse characters, and my clothes cluttered the hallway and living room. She even moved a table and two chairs, a television, and my Nintendo system: everything but my bed.

Here was the woman I loved and trusted the most, my Sweet Potato, ripping all my precious toys out of my room without saying a word about what she was doing.

She knows how I feel about my Nintendo system! I thought.

"Sweets! What are you doing?" I demanded to know. I felt so betrayed. "Why are you taking everything away from me?" Through tears that now streamed down my face, I continued to question her. "How can you do this! You wouldn't hurt me, so why is this happening?"

She kept moving, gathering all the loot together in a couple of big piles in the hallway and the living room. Then she turned to me and said, "Tyler, I just took everything you own out of your room, but there's one thing I didn't take."

"Do you mean the bed?" I asked. "You already took everything else."

"No," she said. "There's something else that I can't take from you."

I took another look in my room, but there was nothing else she could take. I didn't like this "lesson" one bit, and I had no idea what she was trying to teach me. All I could do was stare and cry bitterly.

"There's one thing I can't take away from you, Tyler," she told me. "I can't take away who God made you to be. I can't take the spirit He gave you. I can't take the love you show people. I can't take away who you are or the blessings you've been given or the work God has given you to do. Taking everything out of your room didn't change who you are one bit."

I quit crying and tried to understand why she was saying this.

"You are who you are," she said. "God made you that way, and God doesn't make junk. If substitute teachers or other people don't see you as the unique and wonderful boy you are, that's their problem. Don't you let it worry you.

"Just don't you ever tell me you don't want to be you because *you* is who you are. *You* is who God made you to be. *You* is who your mom and dad love with all our hearts. You can't be anybody else. You're Tyler. All you can do is be you, be okay with how God made you, and do the best with what you've got."

After a moment or two, her comments began to sink in.

"Okay, Sweets," I said. "I will just be me."

Together, we put my room back in order.

I wouldn't know until the next day what my mom would do next.

Sweet Potato Takes Charge

When I left the school building the next afternoon, my mom was standing outside the door. She usually stayed in the car, waiting for me to come to her. I wasn't sure what was going on, and she didn't explain.

She guided me in the direction of the athletic field with one hand softly on my back. As we approached the field, I saw the principal and the substitute PE teacher coming toward us. My heart sank, and I tried to go in another direction. Mom was now patting me on the back as she made sure I kept heading in their direction. I was afraid the substitute was now a full-time teacher and wondered what he was going to do to me. I looked around and saw that most of the kids in my class were still hanging around and watching this whole thing unfold.

"I have something to say to you, buddy," he said as we stood just a few feet apart.

I wanted to yell, *I'm not your buddy!* But Mom spoke up right away.

"Why don't you get down on one knee and look at him eye to eye," she said with an authority that indicated he'd better comply.

"I want you to know that I did not know you were doing the best you could, and I am truly sorry. You are very special," he said with no defensiveness in his voice.

"Thank you," I softly said while thinking, *What did my mom do for this apology to happen out here in front of other kids and parents? Wow! She is a superstar.*

I asked her later how that apology came about. She told me the whole story:

> Last night after you went to bed, several parents of your classmates called me. They wanted to know how you were and said their kids had told them what happened to you in PE class.
>
> Tyler, I was furious. That man should have never called you out like that. I decided right then that I would go into school the next morning and confront him. I skipped signing in at the front office and went straight to the PE office.
>
> I told the substitute who I was and what you and the other parents had told me about the incident the day before. He was young and cocky. He mumbled something about thinking you were just fooling around. His attitude made the hair on the back of my neck stand up.
>
> I told him I wanted him to apologize to you. He remained cocky and said he didn't want to make a big deal out of this issue and saw no need for an apology. Well, then I let him have it!
>
> "You may not want a big deal, but I am making this a big deal," I told him. "I'm going to the principal's office, and you can come with me or I'll go alone!" He came with me, and I told the principal exactly what I wanted: I wanted this substitute teacher to receive a written reprimand; I wanted

> it on his record; and I wanted a formal apology in front of the other students. The principal was totally supportive, so you got your apology, and he got a written reprimand and a notation on his record.
>
> I may not have handled this in the best way, Tyler, but that young man needs to never do that kind of thing again to another student. And he needed to make it right with you and the other children.

My mom might not have been so assertive if other parents hadn't called her, but their calls showed her how severe my humiliation had been. It had upset the other children enough for their parents to call my mom.

The Penguin

There were no more incidents like the PE one, but the name-calling continued whenever kids were out of hearing range of the teachers. For one week every quarter or so, I endured my most dreaded time of being bullied.

Every week our teacher chose a different student to be the "special person" for the entire week. It was an honor, or it was supposed to be, and everyone took a turn fulfilling this leadership spot.

I wasn't very enthusiastic when my turn came around. One of the jobs of the special person was to be the line leader for the week. Whenever the class moved from one room to another, the line leader was the first person in line and the rest of the class followed behind him or her. I hated being line leader. My limitations were highlighted every single day.

When our class was in the hall with me at the head of the line, other classes were also moving through the halls. All the other leaders walked much faster than I did. As they passed our line they'd snicker and puff up like they were doing something spectacular. People would call out to me, make fun of how I walked, and complain when my line was blocking or slowing down everyone's progress. I would just keep going with my head down.

I got used to a lot of the name-calling, but the one I hated the most was being called "Penguin." That moniker was attached to me because of the way my body moved when I walked. I kind of lurched forward step by step. My upper body swayed from side to side like a penguin. While these little animals are adorable in a zoo, there was nothing adorable about being given that name in elementary school.

I'd try to remember my mom's words when she emptied my room of everything but the bed. God made me to be me, and I'm not junk. Boy was that hard to do during those weeks of being the "special person."

Seeking Approval

I was just as desperate for approval as the rest of the kids, but other than the occasional friend who accepted me just the way I was, I experienced never-ending rejection. In PE class

I was always last to be picked. In the case of school dances, I was never picked at all.

In the fifth grade, we had our first school dance. I knew this would be a challenging setting, but I wanted to go and dance with a girl other than my little sister. My movements were awkward, but I could manage. I wouldn't knock anybody down or step on my partner's toes.

So I screwed up my courage and went. The gym was full of kids. I wandered over to the corner where all the boys huddled together. The girls were in another corner across the gym. There was a girl in my class (I'll call her Suzy) who was really cute and was always nice to me. I scanned the group of girls, looking for her long blonde curls and sweet smile. There she was! She was talking excitedly to some other girls who seemed just as excited. A few of the boys standing near me made their way across the chasm toward the bevy of waiting young ladies.

I better get going or someone else will ask her.

I started to make my way across the floor, aware that many eyes were on me. My hands were sweating and my heart racing. I walked up to her with a big smile on my face and said, "Hi, Suzy. Will you have this dance with me?" She hesitated. Her face grew red, and she lowered her eyes.

"I'm sorry, Tyler. I don't think so," she said as she turned and walked slowly into the group of girls who were watching us with wide eyes. I had unrealistically expected a "yes" as Suzy's answer. I would learn over the coming years that the answer to dancing with me would always be "no." But there

I stood, embarrassed and alone. I took a deep breath and ambled over to the side of the gym. Trying to act unshaken, I pretended to be tying my shoe in an attempt to give myself a few minutes before going back to the group of boys.

As I got older I'd try again to gain a dance partner. Time and again I'd get up my nerve to cross the gym, feeling okay about myself except for one thing: my eyes.

If I could change just one thing about physical appearance, it would be my "floating" eyes. I'd change that even more than the way my body moves or the number of times in a week that I fall down. I just wish I could look right at people, and they could look right back. Instead, anyone looking at me close up doesn't know which eye to look at. Both of my eyes move off to the side, so people can't tell that I'm looking at them when I am. I want them to know that I would make eye contact with them if I could, that I am listening to them, and that I'm not preoccupied with anything else. My eyes may be wandering, but my mind is not.

Mom told me that if I lived for everyone's approval I would die experiencing their rejection. I knew she was right, but her being right didn't stop me from wishing I could fit in somehow and be normal like everybody else.

Attitude Adjustment

Just when I would think I had accepted me as me, something else would happen and take me down the trail of self-pity and whining.

After one of my surgeries during those elementary school years, I felt overwhelmed by the thought of going through recovery and rehab . . . *again.* My self-talk pity party scrolled dramatically through my mind:

Not again!

How many more times do I need to do this?

How much more can one kid take?

I can't survive another punishing round of PT.

I have zero interest in going back to the beginning all over again and learning how to walk.

One step.

Rest.

Two steps.

Rest.

Three steps.

A longer rest.

"Come on, Tyler. You can do this!" my mom said as she encouraged me to get up and get going.

"Leave me alone," I cried out.

"Listen to me, Tyler," she said. "In life there are times when we get to choose what we want to do, and there are other times in life where we don't have much of a choice. Right now you don't have a choice about being in pain. And you don't have a choice about whether you're going to recover from this. Your father and I will make sure you'll recover.

"But you do have one big choice right now. You have a choice about how you will recover. Will you be frustrated and angry and upset about it, or will you choose to accept it and overcome it like you have done with every other challenge in your life so far?"

I wiped the tears from my eyes as she continued.

"I understand that you're upset," she said. "I'm upset about all this too. So here's what we're going to do. I'm going to give you five minutes to yell, scream, spit, cuss, throw things, and get upset. Then, it's going to stop and we're going to quiet down and get on with life. If you don't stop after five minutes, you and I are going for a ride. I'm going to take you to the hospital, and we're going to visit the cancer ward so you can see some people who *really* face some difficult situations in life. And after that, we'll focus on all the blessings and good things we have in life. Okay, Tyler?"

I didn't even need the five minutes.

"Okay, Mom," I said. "Okay."

A Speaker Is Born

I recovered and made it back to school just in time for an exciting opportunity. My wonderful fourth-grade teacher told us about the big speech contest that was organized by 4-H and involved all schools in the state.

"This is a wonderful chance to learn public speaking and meet students from other schools," she said. "I want all of you to work on your talk. It should be two minutes long and you need to tell listeners something that defines you, something you are passionate about."

I knew right away that I would talk about how CP had

defined me, and it would possibly help others understand what kids like me went through every day. Before long I had outlined a speech titled, "Why Me?" that described my disabilities and the experiences I had with people who never quite knew what to do with me.

All 32 students in my fourth-grade class gave their speeches to each other in our classroom. Then each of us in the class wrote the name of the person we thought gave the best speech. The votes were collected and given to our teacher. As we sat and waited for the results, I was content to have been able to explain about CP and what it was like to be me. Then our teacher stood up and said, "Our first place winner is . . . Tyler Sexton!"

What? Me? I was astonished!

I'd never even *thought* about winning. I'd never won anything. It took me a few minutes to absorb what had just happened. My classmates were looking at me, smiling and applauding. I felt so special, so validated, and so humbled. These amazing positive emotions were new to me in the setting of that classroom. I was so used to being bullied and made fun of that I reveled in that affirming moment.

My teacher went on to explain that the winners from each fourth-grade classroom in our school would now compete in an all-fourth-grade competition. We would each give our speech to the entire fourth grade at a big school assembly. The winner of that competition would represent our school in the state competition featuring fourth graders from all over Florida.

Yikes! This was getting scary . . . and exciting.

I had never spoken to hundreds of people before, so my family and I worked nonstop as I practiced my speech over and over for my captive household audience. Mom helped me write out my notes on index cards. Handwriting was difficult for me, and she wrote in crisp print that I could easily read. I'd hold those index cards in my hands and glance at them periodically. But I practiced so hard that I could give my speech without the additional help.

The theme of the speech was simple: "I'm a blessing." I wanted my listeners to learn to accept people who were different from them. Of course, I was my own best visual aid. I talked about people who look different or walk differently or have some other issue that singles them out. These people, like me, are valuable and have gifts and abilities to offer, just like everyone else.

I felt good about my speech, and speaking in front of a crowd was fun. Once I started talking, my nervousness went away. I was no longer scared, but I was still excited.

That fourth-grade experience opened doors for me that I could never have imagined.

To help me prepare for my fourth-grade speech, my parents invited me to practice it at their Sunday-school class. I knew a number of the people in the class, and everyone was delighted to hear me. I felt pretty relaxed and did a good job in front of adults other than my parents.

One thing led to another. After my successful appearance in my parents' Sunday-school class, our beloved pastor,

Pastor Bill, thought it would be a good idea to have me present my talk to the entire church. He called my mom and asked for me to get on the line too. Pastor Bill said, "Tyler, it's important to tell people what you've been through. It's a powerful story and will help people change how they think by seeing life through your eyes."

I agreed to give my talk in front of our three thousand church members. That Sunday morning was a whole new experience for this fourth grader. I was up front with Pastor Bill and was literally shaking as I looked out over the sea of faces. My family was in the front row, smiling and giving me discreet waves of encouragement.

Pastor Bill put his hand on my shoulder, and I began telling my story. For the first time, I saw that what God was doing in my life was about much more than me. He was showing me that He could take my pain and turn it into something that helped other people. All I had to do was be myself and talk about how God and I shared a relationship that empowered me to live well in the midst of my life's challenges.

God's Mosaic

My weakness has allowed me to see the beauty in something I call the human mosaic. If you've ever seen an ancient mosaic wall or floor up close, you can see how it is made up of many, many small individual tiles and glass pieces of different colors that work together to create a picture.

That's what I see every day when I look around me. I see

beauty in every color of skin God has given His children, with all the different layers of melanin. I see beauty in every different hue of hair, regardless of whether the hair is long or short; straight, curly, or kinky. In each and every person, I see the glorious fingerprints of our Creator.

Sometimes it was easier for me to see beauty *in others* than it was for me to see the beauty *in me*, but I gradually learned to accept myself as much as I accepted others. Sure, it was no fun to live in a body that was in a continual process of being torn apart and rebuilt. It was no fun to experience continual rejection at school.

But God had given me so many gifts and good things in life. I had much to be grateful for. At church I heard the same message I heard at home: God doesn't make junk. I was starting to understand how God loved *me*, Tyler Sexton. I knew God loved everybody, like it said in the Bible, but I figured that was because He *had* to. It was like He was God and we were humans, so loving us was part of His employment contract.

As I began to see things differently, I could see how God loved me, as me, and saw me as beautiful, just as I was. Instead of setting my heart on being attractive or cool or popular at school, I came to see that I was A-OK. Other people might not always see me that way, but from now on, that would be their problem, not mine.

Sometimes when I look at all the people around me today I see so much beauty it's hard to take it all in. This is what I mean by the beauty of the mosaic. Each one of us is a little piece of the big, beautiful picture of God's creative handiwork.

This isn't the way the world sees beauty, but this is the way I see things now. And I'm not sure I ever would have seen things that way if it weren't for my CP or for my Sweet Potato who helped me see the light.

5

FAMILY JOYS AND BUMPS IN THE ROAD

I (Lisa) looked at the date in my Day-Timer and took a deep breath. December 29, 1988 was circled in red with a green bow drawn at the top of the circle. A slightly late Christmas present was about to arrive.

It was still dark outside as I went downstairs for a sip of black coffee. No breakfast for me today. In a few hours, I would be delivering our second child by caesarean section.

Kevin and Tyler weren't up yet, and I was grateful for a few moments of silence and calm before our lives took another significant change. We had been assured that our developing baby girl was looking healthy on all the progressive ultrasounds during my high-risk pregnancy. No alarm bells had sounded during the previous weeks, and I was now at full term for the scheduled arrival of Emilee Jean Sexton.

Excitement bubbled against the rising anxiety I struggled to ignore. Even though I'd passed all the benchmarks that indicate a healthy baby and a successful caesarean delivery, anxiety lingered. The image I carried close to my heart hadn't become a reality yet. Something *could* go wrong. It had happened to us before. Would our new baby have a serious issue that hadn't shown up on any of the ultrasounds? Would she be wheeled into Neonatal Intensive Care for special intervention before I even got to hold her?

The cherished image I longed for the most was of me being wheeled from the hospital to the car in a few days to go home with Emilee safe in my arms. She would be healthy, and our family would be complete.

I prayed to my heavenly Father to calm my anxiety and give my excitement room to grow. No sooner had I offered up that prayer than I heard the sound of Tyler scooting down the hall. A minute later, Kevin appeared in the kitchen doorway with Tyler perched on his hip and a huge grin spread across Tyler's face. My anxiety slipped away as we three looked forward to becoming a family of four!

"She's perfect," Kevin said as I woke up in my hospital room after the C-section. He placed Emilee in my arms, and I marveled at all eight pounds of her. She had a full head of black hair and snuggled up to me with a contentment that flowed right into my heart.

Tyler's enthusiasm at first meeting Emilee filled our

hospital room. He was thrilled! Kevin put him up on the bed, and I gently placed Emilee in his arms. He looked down at her and sweetly said, "Emi."

I know every mother thinks her baby is the most beautiful baby in the world, and I was no different. She was Gerber-baby, picture perfect. I was holding Emilee and just soaking in the joy of having a healthy baby when a nurse came in and said she needed to take Emilee for a treatment under a bilirubin light. I knew what that meant, and anxiety hit me right away.

"It isn't usually serious at all," the nurse said. "It just means that the baby has too much bilirubin in her system. The special light helps move the bilirubin through and out of her bloodstream."

She went on to explain about Emilee being jaundiced, which caused the slightly yellow tinge to her skin. I already knew most of what the nurse said and wasn't anxious about the jaundice. I was afraid that I would be discharged from the hospital while Emilee remained for a few additional days of treatment.

I was crying when I explained to my doctor that I just could not face being wheeled out to the car to go home without my baby in my arms. I didn't want to be carrying the bouquet of flowers the hospital gives to mothers who go home and their baby does not. He was very understanding and promised to do what he could.

Several hours later he returned and gave me the good news. He had persuaded the insurance company and the hospital to let me stay with Emilee until she could snuggle in my arms as we wheeled out to the car to go home. Two days later, we did just that!

Bringing Emi Home

Because I had a high-risk pregnancy, I had been on bed rest for much of the 40 weeks. That wouldn't be easy for most mothers with a two-year-old keeping her busy all day, every day. But for Tyler and me, it turned out to be a special time.

His mobility limitations meant that he was used to sitting for long periods of time. We'd sit in my bed and read, sing songs, and play games. His contentment allowed me to get the bed rest the doctor demanded.

Those months with Tyler were a real blessing, but I now wondered how he would respond after having my total attention for such a long time. He was excited about being a big brother and thrilled when he first saw her, but he was also a toddler who might have felt some jealousy at the arrival of another little person needing Mom's attention. I need not have been concerned.

Tyler never displayed a smidgen of jealousy. He and Emilee bonded from day one. Holding her was the joy of his life. And he was a willing helper to me. When I needed to do something that required two hands, like managing laundry or making dinner, I could position Emilee in Tyler's arms. He would sit confidently on the floor or in a chair near me and love on his little sister until I thought he might rub the hair off her head from so much gentle touching.

A Defender

As Emilee grew up, she began to understand that her big brother wasn't able to do some of the things she could do. She had mastered simple tasks like tying her shoelaces while I still had to help Tyler tie his own laces. He wore braces so he could walk while she could run and jump and scurry around with ease and no extra support.

When they were a little older and would be out around other children, Emilee became Tyler's defender. If someone on the playground at school made fun of her brother, Emilee would step up and end the teasing immediately.

Tyler wasn't the only one Emilee defended. If she saw another child being made fun of for any reason, she would get right in the bully's face and let him or her know it was not okay to be cruel. The force of her attitude for justice gave her great strength. Tears would well up in her eyes, and her wild, long black hair would whip around her face as she defended Tyler or anyone being bullied.

She not only defended him, but she challenged him too. I remember the day that Tyler went to get his driver's license. During the road test, he hit one of those orange cones and failed to get his license. He was in the kitchen with me later, bemoaning how eager he was to drive and how he deserved to pass the test even though he hit a silly cone. Emilee popped in and hopped up on the counter.

"Excuse me!" she spouted to Tyler. "I'm sorry this is bad for you, but I had plans tonight that you would drive me and pick up my friends, so this is bad for me, too!"

Silence filled the kitchen for about 15 seconds, and then we all burst out laughing. Emilee had effectively reminded Tyler that he was not the only one who ever felt bad. He was, and is, a better person because of his sister. And to this day, Emilee has a passion for justice that started to develop when her brother needed her.

So Far, So Good

After bringing Emilee home from the hospital, I was eager to get moving and take back control of my life. I considered our home and the care of the children my domain while Kevin worked long and hard to provide the finances for our growing family.

Our extended family and many of our friends had their own busy lives to manage. They helped out when they could, but I was basically alone most of the time during the day and early evening. I had to figure out new ways to accomplish basic routines.

Having had a C-section meant that I could not pick Tyler up until my body had healed from the surgery. A simple thing like giving him a bath presented a challenge in need of a creative approach. He couldn't climb into the tub by himself, and I couldn't lift him into the tub. On his own, he would have just slid onto the hard surface of the bottom of the tub and slipped around in the water. So I took an empty Styrofoam egg carton and put it in the tub with water in it. I'd help him get ready on the side of the tub, hold his hand, and then he would slide on into the tub and land on the egg carton. It was a soft, yet sturdy, landing area and gave him some stability to sit upright. This may sound a bit crazy, but it worked.

We got through those very early years one day at a time, and I felt pretty competent about handling our growing family.

Where's the Guidebook?

As the children got older, life's challenges grew a bit more complicated. I'd look for information on how to raise a child with limitations while also raising an active toddler. There wasn't much helpful advice.

Many families share commonalities as well as advice, but we didn't have much in common with other families we knew. Kevin and I would joke about writing a guidebook for people raising an active toddler and a child with special needs at the same time. We didn't write that book but just kept plodding along day by day.

Sometimes circumstances would all but overwhelm me, and then God would send help in unexpected ways.

One of those ways happened one day when I ventured out

to the mall with both children. Tyler was in his wheelchair and Emilee was in her stroller. I was helping Tyler maneuver the wheelchair and pushing the stroller at the same time. The wheels of the wheelchair and stroller got locked together.

I struggled for almost a half hour to untangle them. Sweat was pouring down my face; I was on my hands and knees with my hair falling in my face; I was conscious of holding up foot traffic as people streamed around us; and my frustration grew with every unsuccessful attempt to disengage the wheels. Emilee was starting to squirm in her stroller and Tyler was beginning to worry about what we would do if this scene continued.

"Do you need some help, young lady?"

I looked up through the damp strands of my hair to see an older man smiling down at me. I started crying. Then he patted me on the shoulder and said, "Don't worry, honey. My wife will help you while I move this mechanical problem out to the parking lot."

I picked up Tyler, and his equally sweet wife picked up Emilee. We walked out to our car, and the man untangled the wheelchair and stroller right there in the parking lot.

God had sent help I didn't expect from a source I wouldn't have asked: an older couple strolling slowly along after dozens of younger, stronger people had passed us without a moment's pause. I didn't have a guidebook to use in emergencies, but I didn't need one. I did the best I could, and my Father met my need.

I didn't even get the names of these Good Samaritans, but

I pray they have been blessed over and over again for their kindness to me on that day in the mall.

Dad's Viewpoint

I (Kevin) was so relieved that Emilee was a healthy baby, and at the same time, I thought, *Oh! I'm the father of a girl!* I just couldn't wrap my head around the reality of protecting a little girl as she grew older. At least I had time to figure that out.

Sometimes when I held Emilee and looked at her perfect chubby little legs, I'd drift back to the early challenges I experienced when Tyler was born.

All new parents learn about sleep deprivation—night after night of a hungry infant's cries disrupt any possibility of deep sleep. But it was the precariousness of Tyler's situation that forced me to live on little to no sleep for the first few months of his life. I simply could not sleep comfortably worrying that he could die at any minute.

Every time I laid my head down for even a short nap, I worried that a neonatal intensive care unit doctor would wake me up and deliver the sad news that our prayers and the medical care had failed, that Tyler had died.

I became so involved in the drama of our sick child that I couldn't think too much about anything else. I feel like I sleepwalked through my days, my time at work, and my frequent trips to hospitals and doctors' offices with Tyler and Lisa.

We quickly learned that other people were not going to

be able to help us very much, even if they wanted to. Our friends at church were well meaning, but they just didn't know what to say or do. Some would change the subject when I talked about Tyler. Others would excuse themselves and walk away or avoid us altogether.

One morning at Sunday school, I was in an adult class where the leader was taking prayer requests. One woman told the class her mother had a cold. We all agreed to pray for her mother. One man told us he lost his dog and requested prayer for that. I took a dim view of these mundane prayer requests.

How can these people ask God for simple things like healing from a cold or finding a dog when my son is in horrible pain? I asked myself. In time, I pulled back from classes and small groups where I would experience such feelings, and instead I focused on worshiping God in bigger church settings where things were safer.

Most people I knew showed zero empathy for what we were going through. My brother Ken was the only person I could share my heart with. He always listened to me, encouraged and sympathized with me, and said things like, "Wow, I never imagined what you are going through." I appreciated the fact that he never tried to give me advice, as so many others had tried to do.

I felt like life was full of noise: Doctors were always asking me impossible questions, medical machinery was always beeping, insurance companies were always saying they wouldn't pay for Tyler's medical care. Lisa answered most of the doctor's questions while I came in and out on the details being discussed. I tried to help with the insurance issues, but I was working every day. I knew I had to get some kind of balance in my life.

To quiet the barrage of noise that surrounded me every day, I learned to take a little time for myself. I love riding my bicycle, and some days I would get on a trail and ride for 15 to 20 miles, enjoying the quiet, the exercise, and the temporary experience of calm.

I was brought back to the present when Emilee woke up in my arms. Yes, our family was growing, and the challenges of having another newborn were a lot more simple this time around.

Serious Decisions

Daily challenges, big and small, crossed our paths in much the same way any family encounters growth. Decisions were made about schools and classes, friends, and decorating a pre-teen boy's room in a décor more fitting for him. Plain painted walls replaced walls covered with baby blue basketball designs, and real leather basketballs replaced little plastic balls and toys. Those kinds of decisions were reached with a minimum of stress.

We found ourselves faced with weightier issues concerning the ongoing treatments for Tyler as he grew and his body and his desires grew with him. He still wanted to play basketball and live without pain nagging at him every day.

Medical research and technology discovered new and more sophisticated ways to treat a wide range of conditions, including cerebral palsy. How could the arms and legs of children with CP function with more strength and flexibility? How drastic would solutions be and how successful? The medical community wrestled with answers to these questions, and we wrestled with what risks to take in the hope that Tyler's dreams could be fulfilled, or at least partially realized.

At about age 12, Tyler was experiencing muscle spasms in his legs. A new procedure was proving successful in some cases. Botox would be injected into the patient's legs, and the muscle spasms would calm down. The treatment involved 20 injections in each leg, repeated a number of times. The cost was prohibitive, and our insurance wouldn't cover it. But Kevin and I (Lisa) decided to give it a try and figure out a way to pay for it.

We checked Tyler into Orange County Children's Hospital, and we stayed at a Ronald McDonald House for families of patients. The arrangement was less than ideal, but we didn't have the money to stay in a regular hotel. The next day the chief of the hospital came to see Tyler. He examined Tyler and talked with him for a fairly long time. We watched and listened as Tyler enthusiastically engaged with the doctor and wondered at the doctor's growing interest in Tyler.

After an extensive visit with Tyler, the doctor turned to us and shared about his family. He and his wife had three little girls. One of their primary challenges and concerns was with their four-year-old daughter who was autistic. Tyler's attitude about his own condition and his optimistic view of life impressed the doctor so much that he wanted his daughter to spend some time with Tyler.

Three hours later we were all packed up and driving to the doctor's home to stay with his family. The doctor's wife was a cardiologist, and there we were in a beautiful setting, with two doctors and a little girl who struggled with her own limitations in life.

Tyler and this precious little girl bonded right away. He sat on the floor and played with her, laughed with her, and gave her brief moments of joy in her troubled life. Her parents were so grateful. They, like us, knew their child would have lifelong challenges due to a condition that cannot be completely cured. We saw the despair in their eyes as they sat and talked with us after dinner. But we also saw the hope that Tyler briefly could offer their daughter.

The four of us shared a respite together as people on a similar journey who are not alone. The doctor's gratitude even extended to cutting his charges in half. God sent us friends in our time of need and allowed us to be friends to them, too. During our time there the doctor asked us an interesting question: "How have you raised such a positive young man?"

This question gave me pause as I thought about what things had made a difference in Tyler's life. I needed to think about it.

Just Do Your Best

We drove back home after Tyler's first round of Botox treatments. His muscle spasms had calmed down, but at that point we didn't know if he would need additional treatments.

The next morning I got up before everyone else, as I did the morning Emilee was born. There had been other predawn mornings like this in the nine years between Emilee's birth and this medical treatment. They didn't happen often, but when they did, I wondered why I didn't spend every early morning at the kitchen table with the Lord. A calming peace washed over me as the presence of Jesus was more real than the absence of His physical body.

I sat at the table with my fingers wrapped around my coffee cup and just . . . sat. Phrases and verses from Scripture floated in and out of my mind with the comforting balm of the touch of Jesus. Time passed, and when the first ray of sunlight spilled in through the kitchen window, I felt renewed.

Another medical treatment was behind us, and we could take a breath before the next decision needed to be made. I thought about the doctor's question: "How did you raise such a positive young man?"

I wished I could rattle off a list of things I did to enjoy daily victories with our children. I can't. Tyler is a positive young man—most of the time. He just is. I've tried to be a good mom to him and Emilee, and I believe almost all moms do the same thing. I'm no better than anybody else. But I can't take credit for anything extraordinary.

I am blessed with two children and a husband who have perseverance and strength to tenaciously hang on to good thoughts when painful things happen. I'm the scared one. I have to work hard to keep my fearful thoughts at bay.

Those mornings like the early ones with Jesus are what bring my mind back to the truth. The truth is that God loves me and loves my family with an unconditional love that never quits. He hears us and understands. He knows our frailty. He forgives us. I don't understand why some things happen and some other things that we long for do not, but I do understand the heart of God.

When we seek His counsel, pray, nurture our relationship with Him in His Word, seek the counsel of wise people, and then do the best we can, He tells us, "Well done, good and faithful servant."

I don't spend every morning getting up before the sun to sit with Jesus. My human nature interrupts my good intentions with the enticement of another hour of sleep. Sometimes I feel guilty, and sometimes I just accept the reality of a busy life and limited energy. I'm so grateful we aren't called to be perfect. Maybe what we are called to do is just do the best we can.

6

FACING MY REAL LIFE

I (Tyler) was too slow to be a good baseball player. I couldn't always hit the ball, and more than once I took a big swing, missed, and fell down from the effort. Even when I did hit the ball, I could rarely move fast enough to outrun the throw to first base.

"You're out!" the umpire would yell.

Dodge ball was fun, but I couldn't dodge fast enough to escape all the volleyballs traveling in my direction at very high velocities. My fellow students knew to aim for my legs because if they hit me there, I would tumble over like a bowling pin.

My favorite sport was something we played in physical

education class. Our teacher, Mr. Pike, called it tennis ball baseball. It was basically like baseball, but we used a soft, bouncy tennis ball instead of a hard, heavy baseball, and we hit the tennis ball with a tennis racket, which we swung just like a baseball bat.

When I was able to connect my racket with that yellow fuzzy ball, it seemed to soar through the air for miles, allowing me to get to base safely with my clumsy style of running. Whenever Mr. Pike told our PE class we were going to play tennis ball baseball, I knew I was going to have some fun.

Except for one day. I was walking with a group of friends and fellow students as we were heading to the baseball diamond for a brief game. As usual, I was bringing up the rear of our small group.

As I walked along, I was trying hard to keep up, getting excited about our game, and mostly ignoring the ground where I was walking. That's when it happened. As our group passed by a big cypress tree, I stumbled over a tree root and fell to the ground with a heavy thud. I knew right away this fall was a bad one.

Uggghhhh! I said to myself as I landed. *This hurts really bad.*

"Tyler," one of my friends said, "are you okay?"

"Yeah, I'm okay," I said, laughing it off as I quickly tried to jump up and walk it off. But I could tell.

No, I am definitely not okay.

I wasn't going to let my friends know how not-okay I was, but each little step I took was excruciating.

"I'll be right there!"

No, I won't be right there. I can't even move!

"It's no big deal," I said, crying silently to myself as I saw my knee starting to turn red and swell.

I could barely walk. My classmates were out of sight by now, so I just stopped and leaned against a tree.

I can't even get through one day without my CP ruining it!

As I leaned against that tree, my anger and frustration rose up inside me. *Just one day, God! Please, just give me one day when I don't feel ashamed, embarrassed, lonely, and frustrated!*

The rest of the day I limped around and kept my head down. It was a Friday, and Friday nights were "Family Fun Nights" at home. I knew this fun night would be ruined with a trip to the emergency room.

I'm not going to tell Mom and Dad. I can make them think I had a really active day at school and was just super sore.

Family Fun Night happened, but it wasn't easy ignoring the pain. I could tell Mom was watching me as I struggled getting in and out of chairs and limped throughout the weekend. Finally on Monday, she confronted me.

"Okay, Tyler," she said firmly, "what's wrong with your knee?"

I owned up to my attempt to hide my injury. At that 72-hour mark, my lie was unraveling. Instead of going to school, we took the familiar route to the doctor's office. The diagnosis was a broken kneecap. I went home in a brace and using crutches.

Accepting Reality

God didn't answer my prayer of experiencing life like the rest of the kids. In fact, I became aware that the abnormality of ongoing surgeries would continue.

By the time I entered middle school, I had survived more than a dozen major surgeries. Each procedure I endured had its own *before* period and its own *after* period. Sometimes preparation and recovery were short and simple. Other times, weeks of painful preparation were followed by weeks of painful recovery and physical therapy.

The actual surgeries came and went seemingly quickly. Some required hours, but the anesthesia made it feel like they happened in seconds.

Then it was *after* time. Time now for rest and recovery, although the weeks or months of painful therapy didn't feel much like resting.

Each surgery required me to relearn how to walk, how to sit up, or how to use other parts of my body, leading to pain, frustration, and many more falls.

"Does it hurt a lot after a surgery?" a classmate asked me one day in a kind but cautious voice.

"Yeah, it does hurt," I said. "Mostly the PT I have to do is what hurts the most. Every day I have to move and stretch and try to get my body to do stuff it wasn't able to do before a surgery."

"What do you do when you are absent so much after surgeries? Do you get to play or have any fun?" he asked.

"I don't get to play, like on the basketball court or anything real physical," I told him. He shook his head in sympathy, so I kept on telling him what I did. Most of my time was spent in PT or staying caught up on homework. My dad played Nintendo games with me, and my mom and sister would watch TV with me.

The look on my classmate's face told me that he couldn't understand how I lived through such a seemingly boring life. I was grateful he was brave enough to talk with me and also grateful that my recovery time wasn't boring to me.

When I was younger I knew more surgeries would come, but I kept hoping the next one would be the last. By the time I was in middle school, I accepted the reality that many more might follow. CP is complicated. I'd had multiple surgeries on my legs, knees, and eyes, and I'd undergone countless procedures to correct one body part or another. The goal of all of these invasions to my body was, first, for me to walk and, second, for me to walk with more stability. I desperately wanted to reach that goal, so I paid the price of living a life unlike the kids around me.

Two of the surgeries were more complicated and risky than the others: a selective dorsal rhizotomy and a heel cord surgery. Good results meant that my body would function in better ways and my ability to walk would improve. Bad results meant permanent paralysis and/or impotency. Fortunately, both surgeries were successful!

I used to think that surgeries punctuated my real life, but now it was more like real life punctuated my surgeries. I was learning to face the reality that my real life just would never be like other kids'. No matter how many surgeries I would have, I would never walk without swaying like a penguin or run fast or dance gracefully. *My* real life included surgeries, name-calling, falling down, and continued humiliation.

More Humiliation

I was certainly used to spending time recovering in the hospital. But as a teenager, some of the help I needed grew more and more humiliating. After one intensive surgery, I was in a split cast all the way up both legs.

I needed help to go to the bathroom. Here I was, a teenage boy, needing help from nurses with this most private bodily function. I would lie in the bed in agony. Instead of pushing the buzzer for the nurse as soon as I realized I had to go, I'd lie there as long as possible. My humiliation tortured me. No matter what I told myself about how normal this was and how the nurses helping me didn't think anything of it, the consuming thought of asking for help to go to the bathroom breathed life into my every negative emotion. I felt powerless. I had even less control over my body than I normally did.

Of course, each time I finally hit that buzzer. The worse humiliation would have been to wet the bed.

When I went home, still with both legs casted, my dad would help me. That was so much better, but I hated that he would have to drive home from work during the day if

ler was born
ematurely
nd nearly died.
fter three long
onths in a
eonatal unit,
e was finally
rong enough
go home with
s parents.

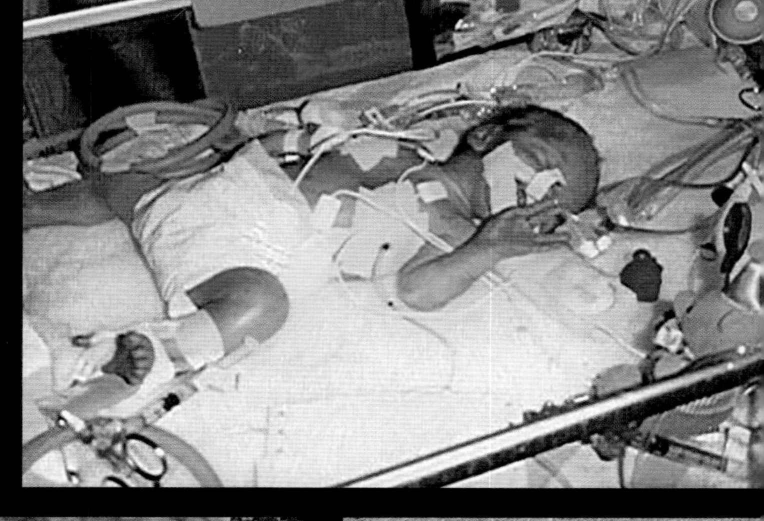

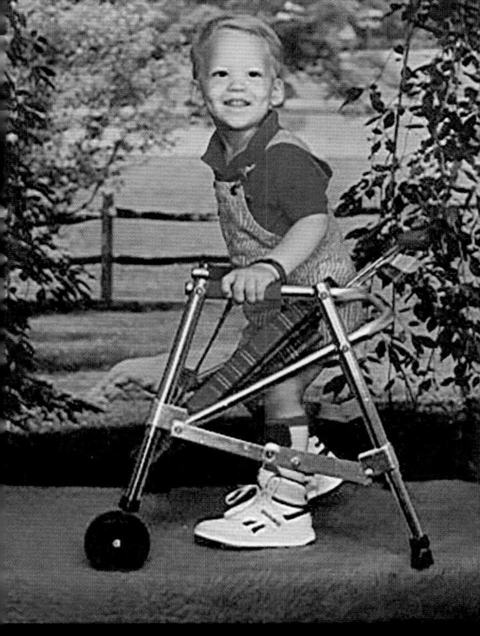

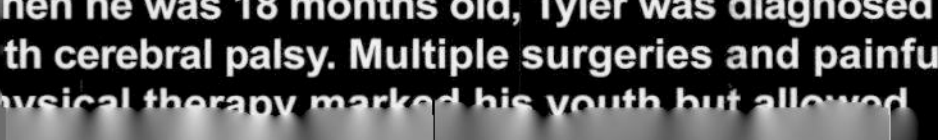

hen he was 18 months old, Tyler was diagnosed
th cerebral palsy. Multiple surgeries and painful
ysical therapy marked his youth but allowed

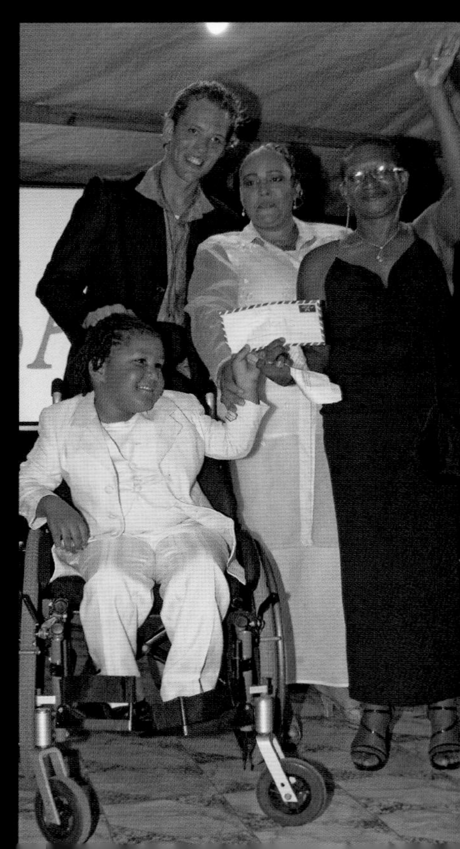

Tyler attended medical school on the Caribbean island of Statia, where he met a boy named Christopher (above, in pool) who also had cerebral palsy. How Tyler helped Christopher get the care he needed changed the island people's attitude toward people with disabilities. The situation also confirmed Tyler's calling to be a pediatrician.

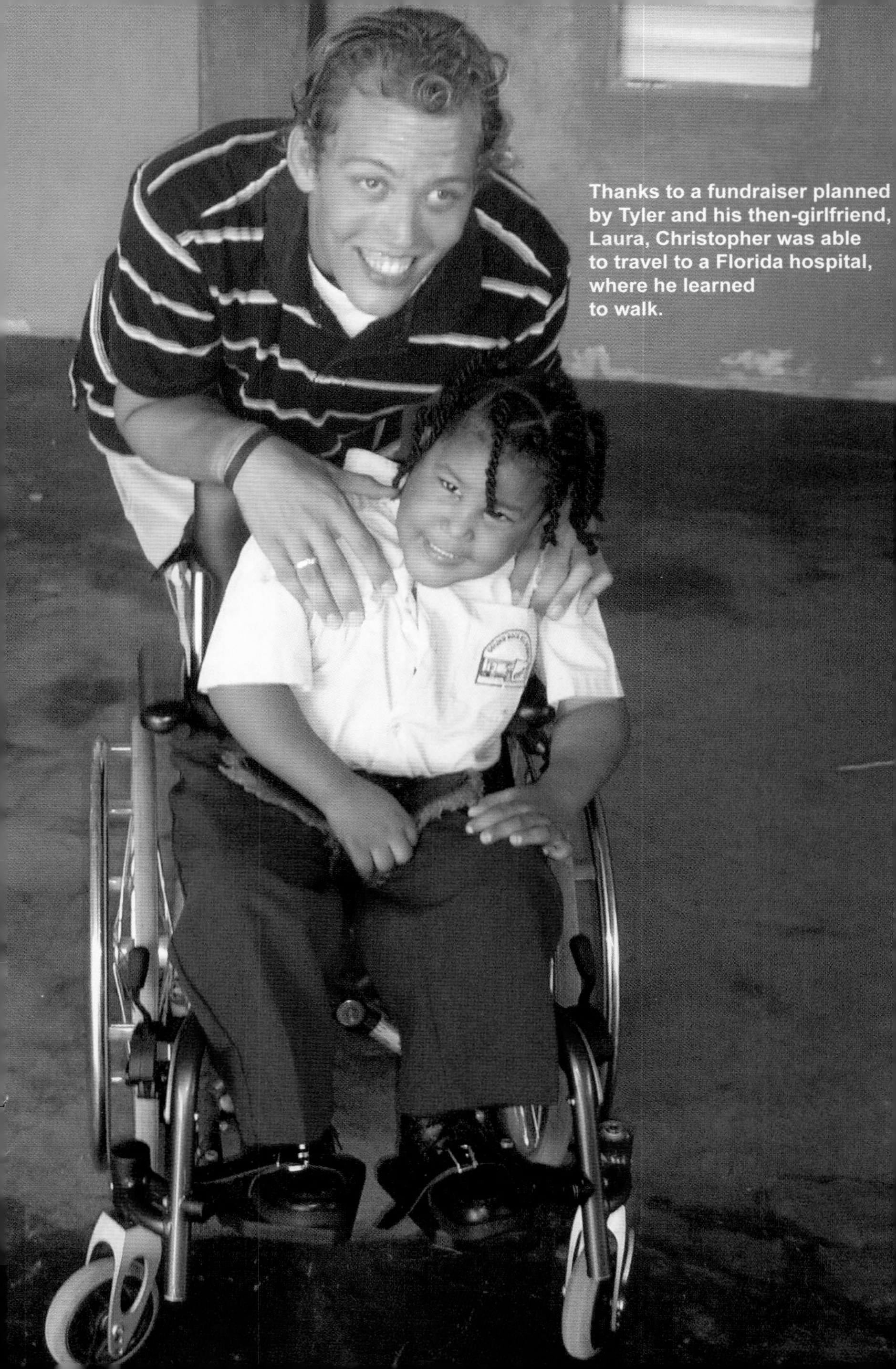

Thanks to a fundraiser planned by Tyler and his then-girlfriend, Laura, Christopher was able to travel to a Florida hospital, where he learned to walk.

yler and Laura on their wedding day (left), and with Harper Grace (top). The entire family (above, L to R): Emilee, Lisa, Kevin, Tyler, Harper Grace, and Laura.

Tyler and his mom, Lisa, otherwise affectionately known as “Sweet Potato.”

Tyler shared a special bond with his first service dog, Danny, pictured here.

Tyler was determined to learn how to scuba dive. His passion led to his specialization in hyperbaric medicine, which treats decompression sickness.

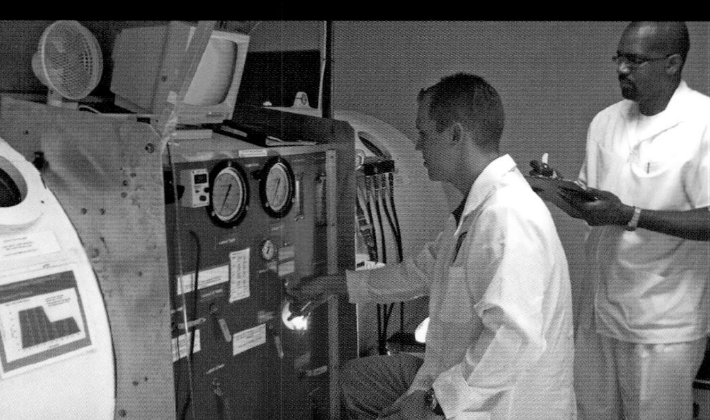

Tyler at work with the specialized equipment used in hyperbaric medicine.

Tyler and his “superhero” team at Singing River Hospital in Mississippi, where he serves as chair of pediatrics.

Tyler speaks often to broaden acceptance of people with disabilities. Right and clockwise: at the Focus on the Family broadcast, on the *20/20* TV show, and at the 2018 National American Medical Student Association conference.

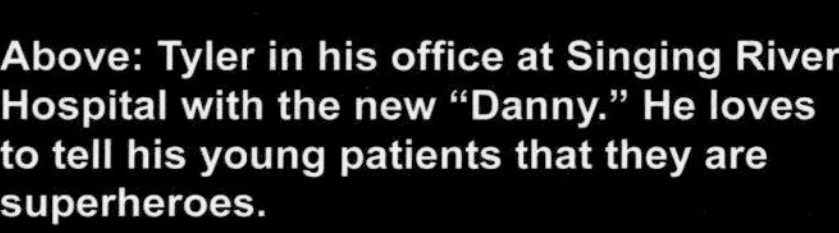

Above: Tyler in his office at Singing River Hospital with the new "Danny." He loves to tell his young patients that they are superheroes.

I needed him. I was just too old to have my mom help. My dad was willing and faithful. I was so grateful to him and so grateful that my middle-school classmates didn't know the extent of the help I needed all those weeks I was out of school.

The "Cute" Ones

I remember the crystal clear memories of one Labor Day watching the Jerry Lewis annual Muscular Dystrophy Association Telethon. I watched it for hours and was excited to see people with disabilities highlighted *in good ways* on national television for everyone to see. It was inspiring to see these kids being special for that one moment.

As I watched the show that particular year, I noticed something changing. I was getting older, but the kids on TV were not. They remained perpetually little, young, and cute. I used to be young and cute. My Sweets dressed me in clothes any little boy would have been proud to wear, and spotless white sneakers always finished off my outfits. But now I didn't look young and cute anymore.

I understand that darling images of attractive young people with disabilities can help fund-raising, which can help fund research for cures and treatments for various diseases. Funding is important because about one in five Americans, or nearly 60 million people, have some kind of disability, according to the US Census Bureau's 2012 report. About half of these people say their disabilities are severe.[1]

More than 8 million people have difficulty seeing, and about 7.6 million people experience difficulty hearing. But the largest group of disabled people is people like me. "Roughly 30.6 million had difficulty walking or climbing stairs, or used a wheelchair, cane, crutches or walker," said the Census Bureau report.[2]

United Cerebral Palsy is the organization that helps people with my disease live "life without limits." UCP uses cute kids on its website and in its materials. I understand that it's good to see positive public visibility for disabled people.

But the use of all these cute kids raises a number of questions. What happens when all these cute little "crippled" kids grow up? Are they still cute? Do people still feel attracted to them? Do people still want to help them?

Not in my experience.

Most of the kids in my middle school would have smiled or been nice to a cute crippled child, but they weren't so kind to the older crippled kid in their midst. I realized that my awkwardness now was compounded with the added awkwardness of being a teenager.

The financial support raised by the Muscular Dystrophy Telethon does help in fighting that disease. The United Cerebral Palsy organization helps many people like me with CP. But I needed more. Those of us with disabilities live in valleys much of the time. We don't live on mountaintops. In the valley of middle school, I needed more resources to cope with life as a disabled young person.

A Personal Faith

My parents didn't have to persuade me or pressure me to accept Christ as my Savior. I wanted that for myself, largely because of the way I saw them living their lives.

Despite the trials they faced raising a son with CP, they always believed God had a plan for all of our lives, including me. They didn't let the doubtful comments from others discourage them in their pursuit of my dreams. They really did, and do, believe in God and that what He says is the truth.

Kids can tell when their moms and dads are keeping it real, and they can tell when their moms and dads are being religious hypocrites who say one thing at church but do something completely different at home. I'm grateful I was born to two people who practiced their faith sincerely and loved Jesus with all their hearts. They live that way publicly, and they live that way privately.

I know some young people who never truly embraced their own faith in God, but God was always very real to me. Faith in Him came normally and grew rapidly. For a while, I was even proud to call myself a Jesus freak.

I loved the music of DC Talk, the Christian rap group that had a big hit with a song called "Jesus Freak." The band also published a book called *Jesus Freaks*. I got the book and started reading its fascinating stories about the lives of Christian martyrs over the centuries. I was inspired by these stories of devotion and dedication, and I decided to follow in their footsteps.

Lord, if these saints could praise You while they were being persecuted, harassed, tortured, burned at the stake, boiled alive, beheaded, or eviscerated, I can certainly praise You while I struggle with my less-than-perfect body.

The Bible started to really come alive for me. One day a verse that I had probably heard a thousand times struck me with new meaning. The verse was John 3:16, which is one of the best-known verses in the entire Bible: "For God so loved the world, that he gave his only Son, that whoever believes in him should not perish but have eternal life."

At first I remember thinking this verse meant that God had just a "general" love for everybody, including me. In time, I came to see He loved me, Tyler Sexton, personally. It wasn't just a generic thing where it was God's job description to love all humans. It was also personal, between God and me.

Another day, it was this passage from Genesis that hit me upside the head: "So God created man in his own image, in the image of God he created him; male and female he created them" (Genesis 1:27).

Again, I went from the generic (God created everybody *in His image, including me*) to the specific: *"God created me in His image. I, Tyler Sexton, am His creative masterpiece."*

I knew God loved me and created me, but reading the Bible also gave me a new understanding of the vast differences between my amazing Creator and little ol' me. My mind was regularly consumed with my personal problems and pains, but God had bigger thoughts. He thought about the whole cosmos and all the people in it:

> For my thoughts are not your thoughts,
>   neither are your ways my ways, declares the LORD.
> For as the heavens are higher than the earth,
>   so are my ways higher than your ways
>   and my thoughts than your thoughts.
>
> ISAIAH 55:8-9

For most of my life I had believed that God had created me, but I thought he had just mixed up the production logistics, leaving me with CP and a life of pain. But now, a new light was beginning to dawn. I came to accept myself just as He created me, without any asterisks or reservations. And I came to accept that His ways were bigger and better than my ways.

No matter what happens, God has a bigger plan and purpose than I can see for myself, I told myself. Looking back now, I can clearly see that was the case.

God Shows Up

The following verses sum up the result of my deepening personal relationship with Jesus Christ:

> But he said to me, "My grace is sufficient for you, for my power is made perfect in weakness." Therefore I will boast all the more gladly of my weaknesses, so

> that the power of Christ may rest upon me. For the sake of Christ, then, I am content with weaknesses, insults, hardships, persecutions, and calamities. For when I am weak, then I am strong.
>
> 2 CORINTHIANS 12:9-10

I had experienced too much to deny the power of Jesus in my life. Weak as I was, I felt strong. I believed that God's strength would continue to move me toward a fulfilling life. I might be called names and bullied and fall down a lot, but God would pick me back up. I would not give in to despair. Two things happened in those teenage years that further confirmed this conviction.

When I was about 13 years old, I wanted to be a scuba diver. At the same time, I was having trouble clearing my ears. That would be a problem for a person diving into the depths of the ocean or even just going to the bottom of the deep end of a swimming pool. But my parents saw my determination, and they never killed my dream. Even though the doctor said I would never be able to scuba dive, my parents got me scuba lessons for Christmas that year.

Well, I not only learned to scuba dive but also became an instructor! God showed up for me beyond what I could have hoped.

We don't always have prayers answered the way we want or answered beyond what we hoped for. But trusting in God and His goodness often allows us to see the blessings in the hard times despite the pain. I certainly don't experience that trust and awareness of God's goodness easily, but it's the foundation of my faith.

I got what I needed as a disabled teen from my relationship with God. That may seem difficult to understand, but it's the truth.

An Accidental Witness

I couldn't wait to get my driver's license. When I turned 16, I earned that special pass to freedom and sat behind the wheel of a Land Rover Freelander. Now I had a chance to be like the other kids in a significant way: I could go places without having to get a ride or be chauffeured by my parents.

I was a new driver and excited to drive to Best Buy and get a new game. Driving in the middle lane of a busy highway, I was elated. The car on my left suddenly sped up and came into my lane, cutting me off. I swerved to the right to get out of his way and clipped another car. Before I knew what happened, my car was rolling over sideways.

"Jesus!!" I yelled aloud. "Help me!"

Strapped to my seat, I flailed around with my arms and legs smashing into the car door, the roof, the dashboard. It happened so fast that I didn't have time to grasp how badly my car had crashed in the middle of that busy highway. Three rolls later it finally rocked to a stop. I was suspended upside down, dangling from my seatbelt. As I released the seatbelt I could hear the sound of sirens growing louder. The EMTs surrounded the car and broke my window as soon as they saw me.

"Stay still, young man," a deep voice said calmly. "You're paralyzed."

"No, sir," I said back to him. "I'm not paralyzed. I have CP."

He seemed a little surprised that I was so calm.

I went on to tell him my name and my mom's cell phone number. While they were putting me on the stretcher I could hear my mom's voice over a policeman's phone. She was yelling in a frantic voice, and I kept saying, "Tell her I'm okay. Tell her I'm okay."

I don't know if he told her.

As soon as I was secured in the ambulance, the calm I had felt began to slip away. My heart started to race, and I began to sweat. I looked at the EMT sitting next to me,, monitoring my vital signs and said, "Will you pray for me?"

"I'm sorry, but I used to believe in God and in praying," he told me in a sobering tone, "but I don't believe in any of that anymore. I'm a pagan now, and I don't believe in miracles. But honestly, you should not have gotten out of that car. It's completely totaled."

My own anxiety was instantly gone. In my weakness, God gave me an open door and helped me go right through it.

"May I tell you some of my story?" I asked this unbelieving man.

He agreed, and I began to tell him how God had brought me through so many surgeries and how He had proved to be loving and kind to me. I had been the recipient of so many miracles in my life that my faith in God was solid.

He listened to every word with rapt attention. If my blood

pressure went up during that time, I don't think he noticed. He seemed to forget about watching my vital signs and just sat there for a moment. As the ambulance approached the hospital, I asked him if I could pray for him. God transformed my need for prayer into love and concern for this man who no longer believed in God but was now bowing his head in prayer with me.

Sweets's Story

After everything calmed down, Sweets sat on the bed next to me and told me what happened when she got the phone call:

> I had just gotten out of the shower. The phone rang and a man identified himself as a police officer.
>
> "Your son has been in a terrible accident," he said. "His car rolled three times."
>
> He said that you were alive and what hospital you'd been taken to. I immediately called your dad, and we each raced to the hospital. We skidded into the emergency room driveway from opposite directions, jumped out of our cars, and ran to the entrance.
>
> "I need to see my son," I said to the first EMT I saw. "He was in an accident!"
>
> After I told the EMT your name, he gave us the good news.
>
> "Your son is fine, ma'am," he said. "You can't see

him right now, but they will come out to the lobby to get you when you can."

Dad and I were eager to see you, and we started to pass the EMT and go on in the hospital.

But as we were heading through the door, the man asked us, "Could you take just a minute while I tell you a story? I've been waiting for you to arrive."

We listened as he told us what happened between him and you. The ambulance was four cars behind your car, Tyler, and he had seen the accident happen. They pulled over and immediately got to you, expecting the worst.

"Your son was very calm," he said. "There he was, hanging upside down in the overturned car, telling us his name and giving us your phone number. The fire department got him out of the car, and I got him into the ambulance."

He went on to tell us what you had said to him and how you had talked to him about Jesus and prayed with him.

"Your boy is a hero. With sirens blaring as the ambulance raced to get him to the hospital, he prayed for *me*. I just wanted to shake your hand and your husband's hand. That accident was really bad. He should not have survived. He told me he just called out to Jesus as he tumbled over and over.

"I don't understand all of this, but it's a miracle your son is alive. I'm going to go home and think about all of this."

Mom smiled as she told me that my only injury was a sprained arm. I was more than alive. I was barely hurt! I went home with Mom and Dad that same day. Two days later, we were able to see the mangled car. I couldn't imagine anyone getting out of what was left of that vehicle, but I was out, and I was fine.

Daring to Dream

I'm so glad I learned to confront the impossible early on. I've been able to see so many impossible dreams come true in my life.

I don't know exactly when the dream of becoming a doctor first blossomed in my heart and brain. I told my mom, and she didn't discourage me, but she admitted later that she thought this dream would fade away just as the dream of being Shaquille O'Neal had faded.

From my perspective, becoming a doctor was simply one more threshold to cross. I knew I could do it, and I knew it would help other people. But my parents were caught in a conundrum, and they were not alone.

Many mothers and fathers of disabled children struggle with what to do about their children's dreams. Like any parent, they want their children to dream dreams and hopefully achieve them. But they also know that disabilities can be real dream killers, and they don't want to see their children get their hopes up only to suffer depressing defeats.

My dream of being a doctor had totally stumped my mom and dad, leaving them uncertain how to respond. So they went to the one person they hoped could help them find their way. That person was our beloved pastor, Pastor Bill, who led the Baptist church we attended.

"What should we do about this?" they asked him. "Do we tell Tyler the truth about his doctor dreams, even if that means popping his bubble?"

Pastor Bill thought for a few moments before replying.

"You don't want to take that dream away from Tyler," he said. "I think it works better when you let a kid dream. And then, sooner or later, when they realize that dream may not come true, they will move on to another one. But you don't want to be the people who take away Tyler's dream."

My parents found wisdom and comfort in Pastor Bill's words, and they allowed me to continue dreaming my seemingly crazy dream of becoming a doctor. I wouldn't say they initially offered enthusiastic support for my plans to pursue a career in medicine, but they never attempted to dissuade me from considering this path.

7

BEYOND DESPERATION

I held the open bottle of pills in one hand and the water bottle in the other. I leaned my head back, opened my mouth, and dumped the pills down my throat. I washed them down with a gulp of water. Darkness.

* * *

How had I (Lisa) gotten to the point of trying to take my own life? Isn't that the lifelong question of the family and friends left behind after losing a loved one to suicide? *Why did she do it? How did we miss the signs? Was she so terribly unhappy?* I'm so grateful that my suicide attempt failed and that Kevin and my children weren't faced with trying to answer those questions.

But I had to answer them. Why did I do it? How did I miss the signs in my own life that led me to take such a desperate action? Was I so unhappy that I saw no available relief? As I looked back, I pieced together the answers to those questions and learned how to move forward.

The account of that terrible day I swallowed a lethal dose of pills comes later in this chapter. But first, let me share the journey that took me to the point of desperation.

Losing Control

During the first 10 years of my children's lives, I held the reins of how our family functioned. I controlled challenges that popped up with school, monitored friendships, and maintained the home as a warm, safe, and comforting place where we all sat at the dinner table at the end of our busy days. Kevin and I stayed connected with each other despite busy schedules. It wasn't a perfectly run household, but I prided myself in managing our lives efficiently.

I stayed in contact with Tyler's teachers concerning his special needs and with Emilee's teachers to make sure she was also doing well. Tyler continued to have numerous doctor appointments, surgeries, and physical therapy sessions. No matter how busy life became, it was important to me to maintain a sparkling clean house and prepare nutritious meals.

As Tyler entered middle school, my control slipped from my tight grasp as his challenges took on new obstacles. It's one thing to be a cute little kid who scoots around in braces and uses a walker, smiling at everyone he meets. It's quite another to be an awkward teenager whose peers laugh at him and tease him.

"I don't know how to handle some of this stuff, Sweets," he said to me one day after school. I noticed a bump on his head and wondered if it was evidence of what he meant. He went on to tell me that he had been playing basketball during the lunch break with some other boys. Even though he was not coordinated like the other kids, he could manage to make some baskets and block some shots. Then one of the boys came up behind him and pushed him down. He couldn't get up on his own. Instead of one of the other boys coming over to help him, they taunted him and threw the basketball at his head. Eventually a teacher came out and stopped his torment.

I wasn't sure how to handle it either. As Tyler was telling me this story, one of the other boys' parents called and told me, "If your kid can't play basketball, he shouldn't be on the court." I was furious!

"That's like telling a student who doesn't get A's to stay out of the library," I snapped back at this insensitive parent.

The call ended, and I turned around and told Tyler the next time that happened, he should stand up, lean on a tree, call the kid over who pushed him, and hit him as hard as he could. If he got expelled from school, I was okay with that! Not the best advice, but I wasn't coping well with how Tyler was being treated, especially compared to the kindness he had known for much of the time when he was younger. Tyler was wise enough to know not to actually hit another kid, or he may have thought I was kidding. I really wasn't kidding, but a physical fight wouldn't have been the best solution either.

Similar incidents like that continued—teasing, bullying, being excluded—and Tyler learned to get through these challenges the best way he could at any given moment. He was managing better than I was.

Tension at Home

One of the greatest stressors in our family was Kevin's unhappiness. He worked long hours in a very demanding job. I had no more control over the causes of that stress than I had over kids treating Tyler in hurtful ways. Kevin would come home late with exhaustion hanging on him like a heavy chain. I was already exhausted myself, so we were unable to support each other. We carried our own burdens and the weight of our spouse's burdens as well.

Kevin finally changed jobs, and that seemed to help a little bit. But my frustration and anger just kept growing. I wasn't mad at Kevin. We just had no real connection. I was as busy as I'd ever been with Tyler's doctor and physical therapy appointments in addition to managing the household and the lives of two busy children.

Kevin was working six and seven days a week in a new job he liked better than the old one, but he was still totally consumed with his own life. He withdrew from me and dealt with his pressures alone.

So far, the kids hadn't noticed that the temperature in our home was dropping. Kevin and I never argued. We just kept plodding along, living parallel lives. I don't blame him for not noticing my rising anxiety. I didn't recognize it myself.

Sliding Downward

My old ways of coping weren't working. For years I had overcome so many obstacles by tenaciously grabbing on to a problem and figuring out how to move forward. I studied about CP, researched information on every surgery or procedure that Tyler went through, advocated for both of my children whenever needed, and prided myself on having boundless energy and creativity. The house was decorated for the different seasons or holidays, and I delighted in trying new recipes and enjoyed keeping up my own appearance.

Something inside of me was off-kilter. My mind got stuck in patterns of negative self-talk for no apparent reason. I kept telling myself what a mess I was, but I didn't have the energy to try to pick myself up. I just couldn't make life work the way I wanted it to. I wasn't even sure *how* I wanted it to work. All I knew was that I felt terrible all the time. Little by little I started to do less and less. I wasn't leaning into my pain with

God's help. I was succumbing to the lie of the enemy that my life was worthless.

Many days I would take the kids to school and then come home and crawl into bed. I didn't even drink a cup of coffee because I didn't want to stay awake. I'd set an alarm so I wouldn't sleep all day. I'm not sure why I bothered setting the alarm, because when I was awake I'd just sit and watch mindless television until I had to go get the kids from school. It wasn't as if I intended to do something productive after the alarm clock sounded. I watched so many reruns of *Gilligan's Island* that I could almost recite the dialogues.

I didn't bother to shower every morning and wasn't concerned about my appearance or the way the house looked. The days of the sparkling house and well-prepared meals were over. There were no more loving notes in Tyler's and Emilee's lunch boxes or lighted candles adorning the dinner table. I didn't care about anything except doing the bare minimum to meet the kids' basic needs and presenting a façade of well-being to people I encountered. It wasn't pride that inspired me to keep up the façade; it was my desire to isolate as much as possible. I didn't want people intruding into our lives, asking what was wrong and what they could do. I just wanted to seem normal enough that the kids would be okay and I would be left alone as much as possible.

I lived by the calendar. If I had a teacher's meeting, I'd make myself presentable and put on a concerned face and just get through it. I'd go to the grocery store when there was nothing left to feed my family for dinner. And I'd go to church.

That's what was going on with me. I'd never stopped to evaluate the damaged thinking that caused me to believe lies about myself. I didn't think I could do anything right. I could not please people enough to be *really* loved. God couldn't love me because I was failing at so much . . . and I was crazy.

Solving My Problem

I'm losing my mind, I kept telling myself day after day. A glimmer of hope must have still been lingering in my soul, because I grasped at the one straw I thought might help me: drugs.

Not hallucinogenics to whisk me into oblivion. I just needed something to help me get back to my old self. I never talked to anyone about my problems, but I knew that a lot of people took antidepressants.

That's what I'll do! I'll go to a doctor and pour my heart out. He'll listen and talk to me and be kind and caring. Then he will give me some medication to snap out of this. I'll feel better. Talking to him will help. And the meds will help me get through whatever happens in the future.

My mind was buzzing. Now I had a plan. I called a doctor and made an appointment. I didn't tell Kevin, or anyone, what I was doing.

My expectation and my anxiety were both high the day I

walked into the doctor's office. I expected to feel understood, and I was nervous about being disappointed. I cried almost immediately as I told him I thought I was losing my mind. He listened to me for a brief time and then gave me his diagnosis. He made no notes and offered no engaging comments to help me feel less nervous.

"You're having anxiety attacks," he said confidently. "You aren't losing your mind or going crazy."

Pulling out his prescription pad, he began to write. "Take these as soon as you feel anxious, and you should feel calm and able to function in a little while," the doctor said. He stood up, handed me the small piece of paper, and shook my hand.

That was it. Ten minutes, at the most, and he was on to the next person in his waiting room. There had been very little conversation. He declared what was wrong with me, wrote the prescription, and off I went.

Desperation Takes Over

My plan was not supposed to begin this way. I thought I would feel great having this little piece of paper in my hand, but I felt worse than ever. For the first time in my life I had told someone the truth about how I felt, and he was in a hurry. Or worse, he was bored.

Even though I had the pills, he hadn't really *heard* me. I didn't realize that he was treating the symptom but not the cause of my intense, internal pain. I thought the pills would be the answer to getting better, but looking back on it, how could I get better if no one ever cared enough to hear what was in my heart?

Hopelessness held me in a vice grip. Lies about not doing anything right filled my mind. *If I could have communicated better, the doctor would have wanted to talk more. He would have heard how terribly desperate I felt. It was all my fault. I've become a bad wife and a bad mother.* All I did was wallow in my misery.

I drove to the pharmacy and paid for the bottle of pills. Before starting the car, I looked out over the beautiful scene in front of me. A causeway led to a wooded patch of land called Honeymoon Island. South Florida is peppered with places like that—places with palm trees rustling in the breeze coming off the water and parkland preserved for tourists and residents to enjoy year round.

I was drawn to the serenity of this natural haven. It was the middle of the week, so there weren't many people picnicking or hiking. I handed my money to the man in the tollbooth, and the entrance gate to the causeway went up. I drove over the causeway and onto Honeymoon Island, heading for the very back of the park, and turned off the car.

I just wish I had somebody who knows how I feel, I thought. *I'm so tired. I can't keep going anymore.*

I held the open bottle of pills in one hand and the water bottle in the other. I leaned my head back, opened my mouth, and dumped the pills down my throat. I washed them down with a gulp of water. Darkness.

Another Failure

I woke up in a hospital. Kevin and my parents stood nearby, looking apprehensively at me. Sitting on the bed next to me was Pastor Bill.

I don't remember anything after taking the pills. Kevin told me that a park ranger found me in my car and immediately called for help. Then an ambulance took me to a hospital.

I tormented myself with thoughts of another failure. My plan of getting through life on meds had failed. Now I'd created a mess by not ending my life. I couldn't even do that right!

The staff and nurses at the hospital were very kind and talked to me with concern. They eased my fears enough that I could go to sleep and face my future the next day.

In the morning I met with a doctor who questioned me to see if I was stable enough to return home. I really didn't want to talk to him but knew I needed to in order to be released. After two days of meeting with him, I did realize that he helped me believe that I wasn't losing my mind and that help was available. He encouraged me to talk with someone who would really listen and hear me.

I thought back to waking up after taking the pills to find Pastor Bill sitting by me. He had said that he would meet with me and walk through the healing process with me as soon as I felt well enough. His sincerity and warmth gave me enough courage to call him as soon as I got home.

At that point Kevin and I had decided not to tell Tyler and Emilee about what had happened. They had been sent on a "vacation" with relatives and suspected nothing when they returned home several days later.

Kevin's Response

Most of the time, it seemed that Lisa and I (Kevin) stayed close to each other and did everything we could to keep the challenges we faced from causing strain between us. We did the best we could. We never really fought with each other, and we worked together as a team day by day.

But as the two of us adapted in different ways to our daily struggles, we grew more distant. The tension between us began to build.

I went to work, thankful that I could be in a normal place and do normal things. I worked harder than most people and longer hours, too, because of the tremendous financial burden of huge doctor and hospital bills. On some days, I spent hours on the phone arguing with insurance companies that were claiming that Tyler's care had been excessive. And I often felt that I was desperately treading water, just trying to keep our heads above it.

Just like Lisa, I wished there could have been some kind of manual to guide us step by step through the many decisions we needed to make. But since there was no manual, we pretty much wrote our own.

Frankly, we were less successful in treating our marriage

well. As we got caught up in our own separate issues and challenges, we spent less time simply being together and enjoying each another.

I saw that I had never really realized how draining everything had been for Lisa. She was a mother 24 hours a day, because she often had to wake up at night to take care of Tyler as he writhed in pain. This went on day after day, year after year, and was emotionally draining on her. I simply didn't realize the toll everything had taken on her because our situation was one where you have to pick yourself up and get back into action over and over again.

I was shocked when Lisa tried to take her own life. After her drastic attempt to end her stress and pain, I knew I needed to stand by her and help her get better.

Back from the Brink

I (Lisa) stood with my finger poised over the elevator button. Pastor Bill's office was on the second floor of the church, and I intended to take the elevator up there. Kevin had dropped me off and would pick me up in an hour. No one else was around. The hallway was empty. I was alone.

The distance from my hovering finger to the elevator button was no more than a half inch. I couldn't press the button. I couldn't imagine how talking with Pastor Bill would really help. I might fail again. But I couldn't turn around and leave either.

I headed for a stairway near the back of the building. The

heavy door to the stairwell lumbered open and then slammed behind me as I stepped inside. My feet seemed nailed to the cement floor as I looked up at the long stairway in front of me. Once again I was paralyzed with apprehension of another failure.

Kevin and I so respected Pastor Bill and his wife, Addie. We'd talked just that morning about how amazing it was that they had offered to meet with me and also with the two of us. Now I risked losing this opportunity because of my anxiety. I closed my eyes and took some deep breaths. When I opened my eyes, I noticed a wall phone at the base of the stairs. I instantly picked up the receiver and dialed Pastor Bill's extension. I told his receptionist that I was at the bottom of the stairwell and could not get over my fear of walking up to the pastor's office. She told me to wait there.

A short time later, Pastor Bill appeared at the top of the stairs with two folding chairs and a Bible. Tears filled my eyes as he came down the steps, set up the chairs next to me, sat down, and opened his Bible.

"I'm going to meet you down here today, and every day, until you can climb those stairs yourself," he told me.

He understood! And I did too. I needed to open my heart in an unguarded way to someone I could trust. I didn't need a list of things to do. I didn't need to go home and clean my house or memorize a verse. I'd been deeply hurt by my own expectations of myself that I'd learned from an early age. I had put a great deal of emphasis on performing for approval and paid little attention to my inner life. I had been a sincere and committed Christian but had thought of God in much the same way I thought of others I'd tried to please: that I would let Him down if I didn't perform well.

Pastor Bill didn't try to persuade me to go up to his office. I could just hear what so many people might have said: *Come on! Grow up and get up these stairs! Stop being so emotional.* Phrases like these ran through my mind much of my life. Our culture shouts out messages of achieving and performing and winning. It's hard to just "be" with all the noise about performing. But here I was in a stairwell, sitting on a folding chair with a person who was ready to listen. I couldn't get going or grow up or do anything. I was just being the broken me that I was at that moment.

A Transformed Mind

I'd always read my Bible, attended church, and truly believed that Jesus was my Lord and Savior. I could pull verses out of my memory bank and teach my children about the amazing love of Jesus. But I had neglected dealing with my internal struggle with negative self-thoughts.

I'd done the external things to be a follower of Jesus and did have a genuine relationship with Him. What I hadn't done was look inside myself to face the wounds I carried from damaging thoughts. I thought of myself as always falling short. I could strongly defend my children, but I couldn't stand up on my own behalf. I needed to figure out why I believed lies about who I was, why God loved me, and the way God created me.

It was internal work I couldn't do alone. I needed to rid my mind of negative thinking patterns so I could make room for God's voice and allow it to touch my heart.

I had accepted unkind words as the truth of who I was. Pastor Bill helped me see that there are some people and situations in my life that I can't change. I can be upset and angry about them, but then I need to lay them down and let them go. Negativity had become a burden I carried all the time. More and more, it was influencing my life and causing emotional and psychological damage.

We may encounter difficult people and situations in many parts of our lives. They may be coworkers, other kids' parents or teachers at school, neighbors, family members, or friends or acquaintances at church. To let go of people who aren't good for our physical, spiritual, and emotional health is painful, and there is loss. It's not easy.

I had some relationships that damaged me, yet I desperately wanted to salvage them. My old people-pleasing mind-set told me to not give up on anyone. I wanted to be affirming and receive affirmation. In some cases I tried and tried again to influence positive change in other people. When I failed to help others change for the better, those failures caused me to feel like a failure in *everything*.

I could tell my kids not to be people pleasers, but I had told myself for years that I needed to keep trying to please people even when they hurt me. My thinking about myself came from the wrong source.

Pastor Bill talked with me about a verse that helped me begin to think differently: "Do not be conformed to this world, but be transformed by the renewal of your mind . . ." (Romans 12:2).

I had let other people and the world around me tell me who I should be as a successful woman in this world. In the eyes of some in my circle of life, I had not achieved that goal. I was less than I should have been. Kevin and our children were not in the circle of negative people in my life, but the negative ones were overtaking the positives in my life. As I'd tried to be all and do all for everyone, I'd worn myself out. In an attempt to find an answer to how I could pull myself up and charge forward, I'd put my hope in a doctor and a pill. When that didn't work, I experienced the ultimate desperation.

My mind had believed lies, and I'd lost sight of God's truth.

In the following months, Pastor Bill invested in my life. I talked, and he listened. When I'd drained my well of damaging self-thoughts, he helped me see the Scriptures and the truth of God's love for me. I released long-buried hurts into the healing hands of Jesus. I learned that it was okay to be angry, and it didn't mean I was an ungrateful person. I dug deep into my pain, talked through it with Pastor Bill, and transformed my thinking.

I read the beautiful messages in the Bible that affirmed me as a precious recipient of God's love, totally accepted, forgiven, and loved unconditionally.

> For I am sure that neither death nor life, nor angels nor rulers, nor things present nor things to come, nor powers, nor height nor depth, nor anything else in all creation, will be able to separate us from the love of God in Christ Jesus our Lord.
>
> ROMANS 8:38-39

> . . . so that Christ may dwell in your hearts through faith—that you, being rooted and grounded in love, may have strength to comprehend with all the saints what is the breadth and length and height and depth, and to know the love of Christ that surpasses knowledge, that you may be filled with all the fullness of God.
>
> EPHESIANS 3:17-19

Those powerful words transformed my thinking. They lifted me out of depression and despair. The most familiar of these verses also sums up so much of what I needed to claim. I substituted my name in place of "the world" to understand how personal God's love is: "For God so loved *Lisa*, that he gave his only Son, that if *Lisa* believes in him *she* should not perish but have eternal life. For God did not send his Son to *Lisa* to condemn *Lisa*, but in order that *Lisa* might be saved through him" (John 3:16-17).

God loves me enough to sacrifice His Son on my behalf. I *do* believe in Him. He has given me life forever. He does *not* condemn me.

Pastor Bill helped me let go of the negative beliefs and accept the truth of God's unconditional love for me. My thinking began to change. Reading the Bible and praying took on deep meaning.

I still struggle with the challenges of life, but now my thinking has been transformed. I no longer beat myself up—I accept who I am as God created me to be. It amazes me that over and over again, I communicated to Tyler the importance of accepting himself as God created him to be, and yet I didn't apply this truth to myself.

I needed to clean out some old stuff in my inner being to make room for the goodness God offered me and continues to offer me. When I replaced negative lies with godly truth, I gradually regained my strength. My energy returned, and I was blessed to enjoy my husband and children again.

As you'll read in the following chapters, Tyler did become the doctor he aspired to be, despite how others viewed him. And I'm still alive to enjoy being part of his story. May we encourage you to also accept yourself as God created you to be? You, too, can move forward in life with God's Word and His love, despite inner obstacles or external challenges.

When to Get Help

I might not have survived my suicide attempt—I certainly didn't intend to survive. I didn't recognize that I needed help, and I hid my desperation from Kevin and the children enough for it to go unnoticed.

Now I know what to look for. I know the symptoms of depression so I can recognize them immediately and seek help. If those old mental videos begin to run through my mind, I know I need to make an appointment with Pastor Bill or Addie and talk about it. I know I need to stay engaged with people. If I'm staying home and watching television instead of going to work or meeting with friends, I know I need to ask for help.

If you're reading this and realize that you or someone you know is struggling with depression, call a friend, a pastor, a family member, the National Suicide Prevention Lifeline (1-800-273-8255), or the Focus on the Family counseling service (1-855-771-4357, available weekdays 6 a.m. to 8 p.m. Mountain Time.)

Whatever you do, call someone and get help! The National Institute of Mental Health lists the following signs and symptoms of depression:

"If you have been experiencing some of the following signs and symptoms most of the day, nearly every day, for at least two weeks, you may be suffering from depression:

- Persistent sad, anxious, or "empty" mood
- Feelings of hopelessness, or pessimism
- Irritability
- Feelings of guilt, worthlessness, or helplessness
- Loss of interest or pleasure in hobbies and activities
- Decreased energy or fatigue
- Moving or talking more slowly

- Feeling restless or having trouble sitting still
- Difficulty concentrating, remembering, or making decisions
- Difficulty sleeping, early-morning awakening, or oversleeping
- Appetite and/or weight changes
- Thoughts of death or suicide, or suicide attempts
- Aches or pains, headaches, cramps, or digestive problems without a clear physical cause and/or that do not ease even with treatment"[1]

Please get help if you need it! Don't hide your desperation like I did. I'm so grateful to be alive. I'm so grateful that my husband and children don't live with the weight of a mom who intentionally and permanently left them. I'm so grateful for the love, mercy, and grace of a powerful and redeeming God!

8

MY RIGHT-HAND DOG

My surgeon's voice rang in my ears, *"Under no circumstances are you to climb stairs!"*

I (Tyler) sat in my recliner and looked over at the stairs. Two more weeks of my four-week recovery period loomed ahead of me. Never being known for my patience or my strict adherence to my doctor's orders after surgeries, I got up. I grabbed Danny's harness, and we headed over toward the stairs.

"Danny, up," I commanded my best friend and faithful companion as we stood at the foot of the stairs. I knew I couldn't make it up without Danny's help. I needed his cooperation.

"Danny, up!"

My words met 80 pounds of steely resolve cloaked in golden fur and topped off with piercing shiny eyes. I pushed against him with his harness, but he firmly stood his ground.

"Danny! *Up!*"

"Nope," I could imagine his canine brain messaging to me.

He was not going to budge. We turned around and he willingly helped me back to my recliner.

Later that evening, still in my recliner, I looked down at Danny next to me. He got down low, crawled under my hurt knee, and lay down. I sat there with my knee resting on his back for the next 30 minutes. We repeated this tender ritual every day for the next week or so. Then, just as suddenly as it had started, the ritual stopped.

"What is it, boy?" I asked him when he didn't crawl under my leg. He cocked his head and turned slightly in the direction of the stairs.

"*Really?* You think I'm ready?"

His tail wag gave me the go-ahead. I stood up, and we walked to the foot of the stairs. This time, after more than a week of propping my leg up, Danny stood right beside me, helping me climb all the way up, step by step.

A Long Wait

I was in high school when I applied for a service dog.

The many surgeries and procedures I endured strengthened my body, helping me to stand up and walk. But there was one problem the surgeries could never fix: I fell a lot, sometimes 6, 8, or even 10 times a day.

As I made my herky-jerky way through the world, I lacked good balance and would frequently topple over, bloodying my nose or even breaking my bones in the process. Sometimes I would just lie there in a pile on the ground, with absolutely no way of getting back up until someone would come along and help me.

I looked forward to getting a service dog to help with this continual problem.

By the time I entered college, I still languished on a waiting list to receive this helper. I understood that training these animals takes a long time. But discouragement was beginning to stress me. I'd been on the waiting list for three years with no end in sight.

Then one day in June 2004 I saw the answer to my problems walking my way. I was stuck for six hours in the Houston airport due to mechanical problems with a plane. At the age of 19, I was able to get around by myself, but I still was hoping for a canine helper. Airports are no more fun for me than they are for you, but when I find myself struggling with a delayed or canceled flight, I try to ask God if He has some purpose in the change, or if there is something He wants me to do. I was sitting in a plastic chair when I saw God's purpose walking my way in the form of a beautiful yellow Labrador retriever in a harness. This cutie was still a puppy, so I assumed he was being trained.

The man walking alongside the dog sat down at the gate

next to mine. I approached him, introduced myself, and asked him about his dog, which wore a sign on his vest that said "Working Dog" and instructed people not to pet or feed him.

The man shook my hand, told me his name was Curtis, and gave me a quick crash course on the history of working dogs and service dogs. He explained that he was a "handler," not a person needing a service dog himself. I was amazed at the man's kindness and his depth of knowledge about these amazing animals. He gained his knowledge working for the Guide Dog Foundation for the Blind in New York.

Founded in 1946, the organization is now called simply the Guide Dog Foundation. It has given away thousands of dogs, not only to blind people but also to people like me with CP who can't walk very well. The foundation spends up to $50,000 training each dog, but it donates the dogs to recipients without cost, thanks to the help of dedicated financial donors.

I drilled Curtis with question after question, and I told him about my frustrating experience of applying for my own service dog. The whole time we talked, the dog he was training just tried to sit quietly but wiggled with excitement every few minutes. Curtis continued to give him commands and rewarded him with little pieces of treats when he obeyed. It was hard for me not to pet the puppy, but I didn't want to disrupt his training.

Finally, when it was time for his flight to leave, he shook my hand again and gave me a card.

"You need to call this person," he said. I looked at the card. It listed the phone number for the CEO of the Guide Dog Foundation. I was ecstatic and called the number as soon as I got home from Houston.

"You must have really impressed Curtis at the airport," the CEO told me. "He usually doesn't hand out my phone number!"

I immediately filled out the paperwork to apply for a service dog, and about a year later I met Mike Sergeant. I still had to wait a little longer, but my name finally scrolled up to the top of the list. Mike would be my contact during this process.

At Last

One afternoon I was in my college dorm room when my phone rang.

"Hi, Tyler," a familiar voice said. "It's Mike. Wait till you hear what news I have for you!"

My heart started racing, and hope immediately soared that maybe my wait was almost over.

"You remember the man, Curtis, you met in the airport that day?"

"Yes, of course I do," I answered, excited but a bit puzzled.

"Well, he has raised a dog and been training him, and we are ready to introduce you to your long-awaited service dog," he said with enthusiasm almost equal to mine.

"*And*," he quickly went on before I could respond, "the dog you are getting is the one you met in the airport that day!"

"You're kidding! That beautiful, sweet puppy is going to be mine?" I yelled into the phone.

"Yes, Tyler, all yours."

A Good Gift

I was sitting on a bench at the edge of my dorm parking lot. Mike and Danny, the Labrador retriever, would be meeting me here any minute. I knew I'd better be sitting just in case Danny jumped on me. Good thing I thought of that!

Mike pulled up, opened the back door of the car, and this furry ball of excited energy ran and jumped right up into my lap. He was all wags and licks and body wiggles.

I thought I'd burst out of my skin with happiness. Trying to hug him was a challenge, as he just couldn't settle down. I loved his obvious enthusiasm at seeing me, and I felt a welling up of emotion I seldom experienced. He was a metaphor for the human acceptance I received almost nowhere outside of my family. Even more than a metaphor, Danny was a lively being offering me generous love. My heart felt so full.

Mike gave him a few commands and he immediately calmed down. He rested his head in my lap with his tail still wagging slowly. We loved each other from that moment on.

Mike went on to explain that we would meet for a number of weeks so Danny and I could be trained to work together. After that, Danny would be completely ready to be my full-time companion. It was difficult at first because

Danny wasn't familiar with the way I would fall down. He had learned to help a person remain steady who had significantly more balance than I did. I also fall often and with an intensity of someone who has less control over his legs than the trainers he worked with. My desire to keep Danny overcame my doubt that we might not work successfully together.

Mike assured me that we would become a successful team if we just kept working at it.

"Trust me, Tyler," he said, "and trust the process. I know how to get him to understand what he needs to learn and how to teach you the way to communicate with him.

"Okay," I said. "Let's do it!"

We worked hard and made great progress.

About three weeks into the training, Danny and I were put to the test. We were in the science building at college and were approaching two ways to move to the lower level: an elevator a long ways down the hall or a wide staircase right in front of us. I was tempted to walk all the way down the hall to the elevator because I feared going down the stairs without the added support of a railing. Students sat on both sides of these stairs, reading or talking on their phones until their next classes. They blocked the railings.

Mike had said that Danny was ready for this, so I took a deep breath and moved to the top of the stairs.

I could almost hear God whisper, *Go on. Trust Me, and trust Danny.*

Okay, God. Here we go, I said silently.

Carefully and confidently, Danny walked me down the stairs. I almost cried. The freedom of making that precarious trip filled me with new hope for how I could maneuver through terrain I had never been able to cross before. I could walk on a path with rocks on it. I could weave through a crowded room without falling down because Danny provided a counterbalance for my body. I could climb up and down more stairs like the ones I had just conquered.

Danny looked up at me as I praised him, and we headed for my next class.

Now I knew it. This smart, loyal companion would help me make my way in the world. I could see that God had answered my prayers and met my needs with this wonderful creature, showing the truth of this powerful sentence from James: "Every good gift and every perfect gift is from above, coming down from the Father of lights, with whom there is no variation or shadow due to change" (James 1:17). Danny was the perfect gift for me.

My Best Friend

Many aspects of my college experience greatly disappointed me. I entered college with big expectations that "higher education" would be different from my previous school experiences.

Unfortunately, lack of acceptance and bullying followed me into the hallowed halls of knowledge. My first experience with roommates didn't help. I just didn't embrace the same lifestyle that they did. They'd go out and party until the middle of the night and then come back and wake me up, make fun of me, and taunt me. When they would finally leave my room, Danny would come and sit in front of me and give me the kindest look.

"Thanks, friend," I'd say as I scratched his neck behind his ears.

They're just drunk idiots, Danny's eyes would "say" back to me.

"I'd be so sad without you," I'd say as he nuzzled my leg.

We'd sit like that as I continued pouring my heart out to my best, and often only, friend. He taught me what true friendship means. He was there to cheer me up when I was struggling with negative feelings. He listened to me as I talked about my deepest thoughts, hopes, and fears.

Several years later when I attended medical school in the Caribbean, relationships with other students were, once again, often painful. My loneliness was increased because I was now leaving everything familiar behind, including my family. The only consistent thing in my life was Danny.

When I'd grow despondent, Danny and I would climb into my dune buggy and drive to a remote beach and have a talk. There we'd sit in the sand, looking at the ocean.

"I'm hanging on to God by my fingernails," I'd say as I looked straight ahead.

Danny knew I was talking to him and could tell I really

needed a hug. He'd nestle close and nudge under my arm to make me pull him closer.

"I'm right here, Ty. I won't leave you," his canine language would convey.

We'd sit like that for a while until Danny decided that the pity party was over.

He'd run about 20 feet in front of me, turn around, and then charge right at me, knocking me over in a playful attempt to get me out of my funk. I couldn't help but laugh at his antics.

He was the best medicine I ever had. Sometimes I thought, *This dog is really the doctor, and I just do what he tells me to do.*

No matter where I was, in college or med school, Danny was my lifeline. My non-verbal companion brought light into my life when no human could lead me out of the darkness of despair.

Going Mobile

I couldn't drive a car once I got to college because the insurance was too expensive. I'd done my best to get around in wheelchairs, but they were big and bulky, and I grew tired of getting stuck in ruts or toppling over on uneven sidewalks. I wanted to walk, not roll from here to there in a big, wheeled contraption.

I loved canes, and over the years I'd developed a collection of fancy, handmade canes. They held me upright pretty well, but there was a problem: I wanted to be hip as much as any other young person, but canes were not considered a hip accessory.

Danny became my living, breathing cane. In our 12 years traveling together as a team, I didn't break a single bone. With Danny by my side, whenever I started to lose my balance and fall forward, he was there, standing tall and strong, to brace me. If I started to fall backward, he would brace himself and I would grab on to the sturdy harness around his neck and chest. He seemed to know in advance which way I was tilting, and he gave me exactly what I needed to keep my balance. When we walked, he would choose the safest route and navigate me through potentially troublesome terrain.

To give us a speedier form of transportation, I bought a Segway, a two-wheeled, self-balancing scooter. Danny loved to run beside me when we had a long distance to cover and a route that the Segway could handle.

Intelligent Analysis

I hate to admit it, but sometimes Danny was much smarter than I was. One of the things Danny would do for me is called "body blocking." If you were to come near me to shake my hand or give me a quick hug—or come up from behind me when I wasn't expecting it—I could easily fall down. So Danny would analyze the greatest threat and protect me before I even thought about it. If there were more people in front of me when I was speaking, he would body block the crowd instead of who was introducing me. If there was only one person near me, he'd wrap his body around my legs and knees, and that person would have to run into him before coming near me. Because of Danny's body blocking, I'd be able to initiate the approach, the gesture—the handshake, the hug, or whatever—on my time when I was physically ready. And then I wouldn't fall.

Danny wasn't aggressive to other people, but he knew his job. He would do what's called intelligent analysis. If four people were on my right side and only one on the other side, Danny's face and the majority of his body would be on the right side and his bottom would be on the other. And he would shift his body as needed. So that's one of the things he helped me with, and it changed my life.

Danny had also been trained in "intelligent disobedience." This method of keeping me safe trained Danny to make the best decision at any given moment. For example, he knew better than I did if we could safely navigate a particular maneuver or route.

His intelligent disobedience would aggravate me when it happened, but I learned that following his lead was my only option if I didn't want to fall. If we came to a choice of walkways to take, he could evaluate the two and choose the safest one. His choice might be longer than mine, but he could discern obstacles better than I could.

If I was headed in a wrong direction, Danny just stopped.

Full stop. I would tug on his harness or give a command, but he would just stand still. No arguing. No fussing.

"Nope, we aren't going that way," he said by his behavior. "It's not safe for you."

Campus Safety

Every day as I walked across campus I was made fun of and ridiculed more times than I ever was in high school. I was amazed that college students could be as mean as kindergartners.

One day when I was on my way to a class, a group of fellow students tried to rob me, thinking I was blind. I was wearing sunglasses and walking with Danny.

"Give me your wallet," one of the bigger guys said in a gruff, demanding voice.

"Well," I said, "let's just see what my dog has to say about that."

He looked down at Danny who had moved between this potential threat and me. The other two guys started to walk backwards slowly, sensing that trouble might be brewing.

"I can just say the word, and he'll take a nice bite out of your leg," I said with confident authority.

All three thieves took off without another word. I knew of no such command to give Danny, but I didn't need one. The bluff worked. Who wants to chance that a dog protecting its owner would hesitate to spring into action?

Later on, whenever Danny and I would encounter members of this gang on campus, he would curl his lip and emit a deep, guttural growl. He enjoyed being the big dog on campus.

Saying Good-bye

Danny's friendship was a gift that I enjoyed for 12 years. I knew the day would come when his health would begin to decline. Dog owners know that reality, but we hate to face it.

I was forced to deal with that sad fact after noticing for several weeks that Danny had been limping. He'd be okay one day and not so good the next. Then he had days when he just couldn't get up. I'd call him, and he would crawl to me. My heart sank.

I was in residency in Mobile, Alabama, and took him to an emergency vet. This kind but unfamiliar veterinarian told me that Danny had cancer from head to toe. I called our own vet in Tampa.

"From what you say, Ty," he said, "it sounds like it's time for him to go."

I was given two days off from my residency so I could take Danny to our home vet to put him down.

After I helped Danny into one of the patient rooms at the vet's office, I got down on the floor with him.

"We'll give you a few minutes alone," the vet said.

The door closed behind him, leaving Danny and me for our last talk. It turned out that we both spoke in silence. He was lying on his side with his head and shoulders in my lap. I cradled his head in my hands and held him close to my heart. My head bowed over his muzzle and the tears flowed down onto his golden coat. The anguish of losing this part of me gripped my whole being.

"Danny . . . Danny," I kept softly saying as I held him close and buried my face in his neck. My sobs were silent but retching. I whispered into his ear and thanked him for walking with me through so many milestones in my life—college, med school, my residency, and the first few years of my marriage. Danny was even the best man at my wedding. Lying there on the floor with him, I thanked him especially for his physical and emotional support. I don't know how I could have made it through so many tough challenges without Danny. I softly spoke my last words to him, knowing he would understand:

"You were with me, right next to me, supporting me with the unexplainable bond we have with each other. I'll miss you every day of my life, Danny. I'll carry you in my heart and remember you as I walk with a new companion. I'll love him, too, but you'll always be my first service dog."

God used Danny to help me become the man I was and still am. I was blessed with the deep companionship of man's best friend.

After a short time, the door slowly opened again as the doctor came back in holding a syringe. He kneeled down on the floor on the opposite side of Danny.

"This will take just a few moments. He won't feel any

pain. He'll just feel safe in your arms and will slip into what feels like a deep sleep," this kind man said softly.

He pinched a bit of flesh on Danny's neck and gave him the drug.

Danny's eyes gave me the faintest of a glimmer before closing for the last time. I held him and watched the pronounced pain lines in his face relax and disappear. His body was limp, but he looked peaceful.

His agony was over. And mine was just beginning.

Another "Danny"

Grief consumed me, and it still hits me when I remember those 12 years with Danny. It's true that he can never be replaced, but I did get another service dog that now continues to bless my life in tremendous ways. He's trained to do all the things Danny did with me, and we have a strong and loving relationship.

When I'm out in public, I call him "Danny." He has his own name, but so many people we run into know my story and automatically call out to him.

"Hi, Tyler! Hi, Danny!" are words that greet us often.

I don't want him to be distracted when he's working, so he just ignores those who call him Danny. When I give him a command I just softly use his real name, and he obeys. Sometimes I think he understands what's going on and thinks it's some kind of a game.

Oh yeah, I hear those people calling to me like they know me, he seems to say. *Don't worry, I'll just ignore them.*

I nod and smile at the people, and "Danny" and I go on our merry way.

Giving Back

Having experienced the life-transforming power of service dogs myself, I now wanted to pass on this gift to others. I have a powerful passion to get more dogs into the hands of more people who need them.

Danny's trainer, Mike Sergeant, and I became fast friends over our shared passion to connect service dogs with people who could most benefit from them. In 1982, Mike founded Southeastern Guide Dogs in Florida, which has provided more than three thousand "extraordinary dogs" to people at no cost.

Dogs meant a lot to Mike, an Air Force veteran who had gone into battle with a canine helper. We met regularly for breakfast, and our discussions would always start with dogs before branching out to other topics. I shared my life story with Mike, and in time, he accepted Jesus as his Lord and Savior.

Mike was a friend who became as close as a brother to me, and he was a valuable and mature mentor during some important times in my life. Sadly, Mike died in 2017, but before he went to be with the Lord, we created something wonderful together. K9 Navigators Assistance Dogs is a faith-based charity that fulfills my passion for connecting people with dogs.

K9 Navigators provides service dogs to two main groups:

- Military, first responders, and families who have suffered trauma
- Families with children who have cerebral palsy, autism, seizure disorder, or diabetes

We acquire our dogs from charitable donors, select breeders, and shelters. You may ask why we work with shelter dogs. For one, we believe it's wrong that a dog is euthanized every eight seconds in the US even if it's still healthy, particularly when some of those dogs could live lives of service for someone like me. We carefully acquire some dogs from rescue shelters as our part of righting this wrong.

We select and train our dogs so they can help people in four important ways:

- *Service Dogs* like Danny help people with many different types of disabilities, including autism, balance issues, and post-traumatic stress disorder (PTSD). Some dogs help people who suffer from seizures or people who need to be alerted to other medical issues like low blood sugar. We've also seen how military veterans and first responders dealing with PTSD find that having a dog by their side can help them control their symptoms, allowing them to function in everyday life. Service dogs are trained to ease the symptoms of PTSD. Simply training a dog to walk beside a man with PTSD can give the man the confidence that someone has his back. In some cases, a dog is trained to nudge a man's hand when he shows symptoms of PTSD-like anxiety, depression, or troubled sleep.

- Unlike Danny, *Skilled Assistance Dogs* don't go out in public, and they don't go through the training such social interaction requires. These dogs stay with people in the familiar confines of their homes, helping them with the domestic challenges they face. Some dogs help people fetch things they need. Others wake people when it's time for dinner or pills. Many provide people the balance they need to walk.

- *Companion Dogs* bring loyalty and love to military veterans, first responders, and their families. Many veterans of our wars in Iraq and Afghanistan suffer from PTSD due to traumatic episodes that occurred on the battlefield. First responders can suffer similar trauma when dealing with natural or human-caused tragedies. We find dogs that love attention and affection. Our goal is to help heal the emotional wounds by matching loving dogs with people who need help coping with psychological trauma and regaining a sense of purpose, confidence, and optimism in their lives.

- *Therapy Dogs* are provided to military and VA hospitals, clinics, and other facilities for wounded soldiers. Therapy dogs provide both physical therapy assistance and emotional support.

This chapter told Danny's entire story, including how his life ended. In the next chapter, Danny returns as I tell you about my calling to be a pediatrician and my medical school experience on a Caribbean island.

Those years certainly held more adventures for Danny and me, and they brought me to the place where I would meet the woman who would become my wife!

9

CONFIRMING MY CALLING

I (Tyler) had known I wanted to be a doctor for a long time, but I hadn't felt called to a specific field by the time I was ready to apply to medical school. Looking back now, I can see how two earlier incidents had piqued my interest in a particular field and prepared my heart to confirm my calling.

"Sweets," I said to my mom as she picked me up from school one day during my eighth-grade year. "I need to go visit someone in the hospital!"

"Who do you need to visit, Tyler?" Mom asked as we pulled out of the school pick-up line.

"Alexa. She's a girl in my class, and she's been absent for weeks. I found out today that she's been in the hospital all that time. She's really sweet and cute, and we talked every day before she got sick."

"Okay, we'll go tomorrow after school," Mom said encouragingly.

The next afternoon we took the elevator up to the children's floor of the hospital and headed for Alexa's room. I was excited to see her and walked into the room ahead of my mom.

I hardly recognized the person lying in the bed. She was shrunken into a skeleton-shaped stranger. Alexa's cheekbones pushed up against her pale white skin. Her arms were so skinny—they looked like they couldn't even pick up their own bony weight. I tried to hide my utter shock.

"Hi, Alexa," I said cheerfully.

"Hi, Tyler," she softly said with a weak smile.

That smile reminded me of the Joker from the Batman movies. Her mouth looked like a scar that was too big for her emaciated face. The pretty girl I knew had disappeared. I couldn't hide my shock any longer.

"Alexa, why did you do this to yourself?" I asked as kindly as I could.

"Everyone said I was fat," she whispered with downcast eyes.

"That's just not true," I said. "I think you're beautiful just the way you are. Plus, I always thought of you as one of the popular girls at school, since you're a cheerleader and have lots of friends. Alexa, just look at me," I said. "I'm not perfect, but I'm okay with the way I am. Why can't you be okay with the way you are?"

"Oh, Tyler," she said, "you *are* perfect the way you are."

How could she believe that about me and, at the same time, think she was not okay herself?

That's the day I learned the meaning of the eating disorder called anorexia.

Alexa went to a rehabilitation program as soon as she was released from the hospital. Psychologists were going to help her understand her eating disorder and her negative body image. We wrote a few letters back and forth, but it seemed like she was gone from my life forever.

After what seemed like a long time, the Alexa I'd known before her illness was back. She had completed her recovery and looked terrific.

"Tyler, you're the only person in the school who cared enough to come see me," she said, squeezing my hand.

We never spoke of it again, but I sure was glad to have Alexa back. And because of what I had seen her go through, I started thinking about how I could grow up to be the kind of doctor who would be able to understand kids like Alexa so I could help them and bring them hope.

I was able to give this type of role a test run while I was doing my pre-med studies. I volunteered for the Shriners Hospitals for Children in Tampa, Florida. That led to a part-time job as a Child Life Aide, helping children who had been burned or otherwise injured or disabled.

One day I was helping the staff take a group of these kids

out for a big event—a home game with the NFL's Tampa Bay Buccaneers. The children were so excited as we transported them to the stadium for the big event.

We were all sitting together as a group, and I noticed a beautiful little girl enthusiastically yelling and cheering with all her heart. One of the other aides told me that Anna had been burned in a horrible house fire. Despite her injuries, she experienced sheer joy at that game. I loved watching her and recognized something special happening inside of me.

More and more, I saw how God had given me a special kind of love for these hurting little children. I could see beauty and glory in them that others didn't always see.

My divine calling was beginning to be confirmed and refined by my real-world experiences. I continued to be led in the direction of pediatric medicine. I wasn't totally sure yet, but I did know it was time to pursue my medical degree.

I geared up mentally and emotionally to fight hard against the predictable rejection from many medical schools before finding the one that would accept me.

"Not a Fit"

If you've ever seen the TV drama series *The Good Doctor*, you may understand the kinds of challenges I've faced in pursuing my dreams.

The central character in the show is Dr. Shaun Murphy, a gifted surgeon who has a mild form of autism. In the early episodes of the series, it's clear that some of Shaun's coworkers and supervisors consider him incapable of making it in a chaotic hospital situation. Some argued against hiring him in the first place, and once he was there, others argued for firing him. But Shaun proved them wrong time and time again, saving patients' lives after consulting his mental encyclopedia of medical training.

I know what it's like to be in Shaun's shoes and hear otherwise enlightened medical professionals declare that people like us have no place in modern medicine.

Much later in my journey, I had the opportunity to appear on the television show *20/20* in a segment highlighting real-life good doctors ("The Good Doctors: Brilliance and Bravery," on YouTube).

But I had a lot of obstacles to overcome before making that television appearance.

Like many aspiring students, I sent out applications to some of the nation's top medical schools, and at least one of them expressed interest in me—until they saw me. During one brief interview, a dean at this prominent school told me: "On paper you look amazing, but I don't think you'll fit in here."

What? I thought as he made that comment with a straight face. There was no attempt to soften his remark or even ask me how I felt I could manage my disability and still become a doctor. It was a flat-out *no*! He'd admitted that I possessed the required qualifications, but after one look at me he slammed the door shut on studying at his school.

I've faced all kinds of rejection and discrimination in

my life, but nothing had ever shattered me like the comments from that dean. I expected most people to dismiss and demean me, but I never expected such treatment from medical professionals. Another school offered me a position but rescinded its offer at the last minute.

I thought about giving up, but this wasn't just about me. I was a man on a mission. I wanted everyone to know that people like me, with disabilities like mine, can contribute much to society. I was determined to do all I could to make that case within the medical establishment, both for myself and for the millions of others who are discriminated against because of their physical limitations.

None of the major American medical schools would touch me. Why should they accept me when so many able-bodied students were applying? That explains how I became a student at AUIS, the American University of Integrative Sciences, School of Medicine, located on a small Caribbean island named Saint Eustatius, but which most people call Statia. Let me tell you about my adventures, challenges, and victories there and how I solidified my calling to become a pediatrician.

Paradise?

Danny and I were squashed in the backseat of a tiny aircraft for the last leg of our journey to Statia. I was excited . . . and scared, not about flying in this puddle jumper but about how my fellow students and the island people would react to a man with twisted legs and a big dog. I'd known how to live independently in college, but how would I live in a place where everything was strange? Would people help me or would they shun me? Would we be able to get around on dirt paths and stony terrain or would Danny be perplexed at the unfamiliar environment?

I peered out the tiny plane window as we flew toward the one landing strip. My fears subsided as the beauty of the island lay before me. Statia was a natural paradise. A volcano stood up above the landscape of rolling hills and verdant pastures. A pristine white-sand beach edged the magnificent blues of the Caribbean Sea. The lure of scuba diving encouraged me to embrace what lay ahead of me instead of getting off this plane with trepidation.

There were no services at the airstrip, so the school had ordered a taxi to pick me up. Danny and I climbed into the taxi, and it wasn't long before the driver delivered us to our new address. Along the way we had to stop for a herd of cows parked in the middle of the road. We waited. We waited some more. Eventually one of the cows meandered over to the side of the road, and her companions ambled after her.

The medical school didn't have its own housing for students, so it rented apartments from the local people. Renting an apartment for Danny and me proved to be a challenge for the school because none of the locals wanted to deal with a dog. Most of the island dogs ran free, and wild ones sometimes attacked the local people's goats.

A companion dog was a completely unknown kind of

dog. The locals had no idea what Danny's role was in my life. They feared this new canine resident as much as they feared the wild dogs who came after their goats. One dear woman, Ruth, agreed to risk the presence of these two mysterious renters.

Danny wasn't the only one the locals feared. Some local officials had tried to prevent me from coming because they thought CP was a contagious disease that would infect the whole community.

Thankfully, representatives of the medical school came to my defense, convincing island officials that CP is a static, non-progressive neurological condition, and it's *definitely not* contagious.

Our driver pulled up and stopped next to a lovely house with a garage next to it. My wonderful landlady greeted me and showed me inside my new home. She had converted the garage next to the house into an apartment. The main area consisted of a small stove, a sink, and a little table with two chairs; a back room offered a single bed and a window; and a tiny bathroom with a stall shower completed my new home.

It was dark by the time we had arrived at Ruth's house, so I fell into bed exhausted after saying good night to her. Around 3 a.m., I was startled to hear roosters crowing and donkeys baying.

Am I on Old MacDonald's farm? I thought to myself, feeling groggy and still weary from travel.

As the sun rose several hours later, I stepped out of my

apartment and reveled at the sight before me. Ruth's property was up on a hill and overlooked the sea. This breathtaking view more than compensated for the noisy night creatures and stark simplicity of my new home. The other sight that thrilled me was that of a red dune buggy parked near my front door. The school had arranged this transportation to help me get around and provide the needed additional help that Danny couldn't provide. If we had to go any distance or over rocky terrain, we took the dune buggy. It was a two-seater, and Danny loved it! He'd sit next to me with his ears flapping in the breeze, looking like the Canine King of the island.

Loneliness and Joy

Riding with Danny in my dune buggy was wonderful.

Unfortunately, time with most of my classmates was just the opposite.

"You're never going to make it," one athletically built guy said to me as we were leaving class one afternoon. "Why don't you just give it up?" he continued as he swaggered past me.

Another student told me he would never bring any of his children to a medical practice I operated. Other similar remarks and rebuffs came my way on a regular basis. I didn't retaliate in anger to these painful comments. I just held on to Danny's harness and walked away.

"You're just a fake with no emotions," was their response to my restraint.

Little did my taunters know, my emotions raged inside of me at the unkind and unjust remarks. But I knew that defending myself would change nothing.

The locals were afraid of Danny, so they were not very welcoming either. Life was often tough and lonely, but three things brought me great joy.

On weekends, Danny and I would head to the beach and I'd escape to the undersea world I loved. The crystal clear waters of the Caribbean provide some of the best scuba-diving experiences in the world. I'd spend all day Saturdays, and Sundays after church, escaping the troubles of the week with Danny and that glorious sea.

The adults may have been afraid of Danny and me, but the kids loved us.

"Hey, Tyla!" they would yell to me in their island accents. They'd cluster around us, and I'd joke with them and answer questions the adults were afraid to ask. They'd ask me why I walked funny and why I couldn't look right at them. They were so open and curious without being judgmental. I do walk funny and my eyes do wander. It was a relief to be asked about these differences instead of being ignored or bullied. I loved to answer their questions and take the mystery out of my uniqueness.

I started to have these local children come to my apartment for a Bible study and just to hang out. We would play games and laugh and eat raw sugar cane that the kids would bring. Their acceptance helped fill the lonely places in my heart.

The third thing that brought joy to my life was a fellow student, Laura, who came to the medical school from Canada. We became friends, and she didn't let my weird walk and wandering eyes keep her from hanging out with me. We became study partners with no romance present to complicate our meaningful friendship.

Joy was filtering in between the hurtful remarks and lonely times. I was settling into my life while realizing that I *could* finish med school and become the doctor I dreamed of being.

A New Obstacle

Danny and I were sitting on the beach one day just like many other days.

"Ouch!" I said out loud as I slapped my arm.

Danny looked up at me curiously.

What's wrong, Tyler? I could imagine him saying.

"That must have been a honkin' big mosquito," I said to him.

He wagged his tail when he saw that I was okay, and we gathered up our things and headed home.

A few days later I was sitting in class and felt really strange. Suddenly everything went dark. When I regained consciousness, I saw students and the professor huddled around me.

"You passed out, man!" the professor said.

My symptoms of dengue fever, a powerful virus, didn't go away: high fever, severe headaches, pain behind the eyes, blindness, nausea, vomiting, and skin rash. I was hospitalized on the island, but there was talk of flying me to Puerto Rico where my parents could meet me and spend some time with me before I passed away.

Thankfully that didn't happen, but I remember thinking, *I've come this far and overcome so many challenges only to die from a mosquito bite?*

One of the most troubling results of my brush with death was temporary blindness. The doctor told me that my sight would return, but days and nights filled with endless darkness started to wear away my confidence that God had called me to Statia or even to continue pursuing a medical degree.

My sight did return, and I did not give up my dream. This scary episode receded into the back of my mind with some of the other ongoing challenges.

"You're the One!"

Danny and I were walking down the hill from school to my dune buggy one afternoon when a heavily accented voice called out to me.

"You're the one! You're the one!"

A local woman was leaning out the window of her car, waving and yelling to me. I could catch enough English-sounding words mixed in with her Spanish to understand that she desperately wanted me to come over to her. She started crying and motioning for Danny and me to get in her car and go with her.

"Please come, doctor! Please come!"

I tried to explain that I was just a medical student and not a doctor, but her pleas for help escalated. She apparently had heard about me from the island children. I knew it wasn't particularly smart to get in a car with a local I didn't know, even a woman, and go off to an unknown destination. At the same time, I knew I would go to the passenger side of her tiny car and squeeze Danny and me in next to her.

She pushed open the door and Danny waited for my command. I looked at the large woman in the tiny car jammed with all manner of things and pointed to the floor in front of the passenger seat. Danny obediently jumped in, and I crawled over and around him to fold into the only remaining available space. As I sat down, the car buckled slightly. The woman turned on the ignition as if nothing was amiss, and off we went.

Not far away we pulled up to a small, beautiful concrete-block house. The front door and all the windows were wide open. Sheer white curtains at each window softly waved in the breeze, welcoming me inside.

I followed the woman in through the front door and looked in the direction of her gesturing. A small crippled boy sat hunched over in an antique wheelchair. He faced one corner of the room with his back to us.

His mom managed to tell me her son's story. Christopher was bullied so much in school that he no longer communicated much at all. He had withdrawn into himself, and some school officials thought he was just being obstinate and disobedient. His misbehavior seemed to cause those officials to determine he was "bad." There was no understanding that he was a very disabled little boy and needed medical and emotional help.

"Make him like you," his mom, Christina, said to me. I knew she wanted him to be able to get out of that antiquated wheelchair and walk.

My heart broke as I looked at this four- or five-year-old boy. I could see that he had spastic quadriplegia, a form of cerebral palsy that affects all four limbs. I walked over to Christopher, grabbed a chair, and sat down right in front of him. He kept his head down. I put my head down and gently bumped heads with him. He smiled.

"I'm like you, Christopher," I said while pointing to my twisted legs and wandering eyes. He couldn't use his left hand, and his right hand was bent down at the wrist. I held his right arm up and gave him a modified high five. His face lit up and our relationship began.

"Christina," I said to his mom, "I will help your son if I can get Shriners Hospitals for Children in Tampa, Florida, to accept him for treatment."

God's Plan

After leaving Christopher's home I thought back to all the times since arriving in Statia that I had struggled with being here. Waves of discouragement would crash over me when life was so difficult that even my three joys (scuba diving, kids, and Laura) couldn't bolster me up. These down times didn't happen often, but when they did they almost broke my determination. I missed my family and friends at home. I missed the familiarity of my church community at home. I wondered if I would ever be part of a medical community where I would be completely accepted. I kept asking God to help me be certain that I was on the right life path.

Now, after meeting Christopher, a strong confirmation washed over me instead of waves of discouragement.

Christopher is why I'm here, I said to myself. *I'm here to help change that little boy's life, to give him hope and a belief that he really might be able to walk.*

There's a verse in the Bible that includes this question: "And who knows whether you have not come to the kingdom for such a time as this?" (Esther 4:14).

The kingdom in that verse is Persia (now called Iran), and Esther was there at that time so God could use her to save the Jews living there.

For such a time as this.

As I thought about that phrase, I realized its meaning applied to me.

I'm on this island, I thought, *not only to earn a medical degree but also as part of God's plan for Christopher's life!*

If I had not been on this particular island where Christopher lives, if I did not have CP, if I had not learned to walk, if the island children had not told Christina about me, and if I had not understood the way Christopher felt, only God knows what would have happened to that little boy. Instead, I was now on a mission I never could have imagined the day I climbed out of that tiny puddle jumper.

All my former questions and misgivings about studying on Statia and becoming a doctor were gone. Excitement replaced doubt. I knew there would be more times of discouragement, but confidence replaced my lingering thoughts of uncertainty. I was called to be a medical doctor, and I would complete my studies here on Statia. The negativity from fellow students and some of the locals would only serve to remind me of that little boy smiling at me as we playfully bumped heads on our first meeting.

I needed to start working on the huge challenge of getting Christopher to Shriners Hospital for his best hope to learn to walk.

When I was an aide at Shriners, there were some child-life specialists who worked beside me to help a number of children like Christopher. I called these women "my girls." That first night after meeting Christopher, I called them and asked if they could work with him. They talked to the hospital's administrators, advocating for Christopher. These dedicated women helped me coordinate getting Christopher's care approved and paid for.

"If you can raise the money to get him here," they told me later, "the hospital will accept him and pay for the treatments."

Island Gala

"Where do you go after school every day?" Laura asked me one day after classes, noticing that I'd been disappearing on a regular basis.

"I go to see a little boy I'm trying to help," I said. "Would you like to come along?"

Several days later Laura came with me to see Christopher with her arms full of coloring books and some little toys he might like. I'd told her all about Christopher's special needs and my hope to raise the money needed to get him to Florida.

One evening after visiting Christopher, Laura and I were hanging out at my apartment when she said, "We should have a benefit gala!"

Within minutes we were brainstorming how to advertise the event. Laura helped get some clubs on campus to participate, and I started talking in all kinds of public places about how much more important a person's spirit is than his body. I demystified Christopher's condition and explained how this little boy was valuable. He needed to be seen for who he was and not shunned because of how he looked.

"If we all work together," I told the locals, "we can raise the money we need to send Christopher to a special hospital in the United States. And they can help him learn to walk." People became curious and started to get excited.

My landlady introduced me to a friend of hers who hosted a local television talk show. I appeared on the show, turning it into a telethon. We raised $2,000 from that one connection.

Suddenly my unpopularity on the island had morphed into my being a sought-after celebrity. Local people and organizations donated a tent, provided food, and drummed up enthusiasm for the event. It was billed as a gala to honor Christopher and raise money for him to fly to the special hospital for treatment. We had a band, a raffle, and a dinner. The response was overwhelming. On the big night, more than a thousand people showed up.

At one point our planning committee panicked as the crowd grew larger and larger and the food began to dwindle. I'm not totally sure how it happened, but everyone was fed, and we marveled at the amount of leftovers. As far as I was concerned, the age of miracles hadn't ended!

God honored our efforts in ways beyond our comprehension. The gala raised $9,000, enabling me to travel to Tampa with Christopher and then back again to accompany him home to an eager island community.

A New Life

Six weeks after Christopher's arrival at Shriners Hospital, I returned to Florida so I could accompany Christopher back to his island home. As I walked into his room, I was overcome with emotion. This boy who had once been an outcast on Statia, stuck in an antique wheelchair, was now standing up and taking a step toward me! I cried tears of joy and relief as I put my hand on his shoulder. I'd been trusting God to bless Christopher, but seeing him walk was a powerful display of how God works in people's lives and how He can bring together even those whose odds of meeting are so very small.

A crowd was waiting for us as we landed on Statia. The entire community had contributed to this moment, and they all shared in the excitement Christopher and I felt as we stepped out of that plane.

My life could not have been more different from the first time I arrived on Statia. This time, I was treated like a celebrity and showered with gifts, including everything from a refurbished automobile to a goat. I never had to pay for a cheeseburger again, and photos of the island governor shaking my hand dotted the walls of many local establishments.

All these perks were wonderful, but the greatest reward for my efforts to help Christopher was the fact that other island children with disabilities were now valued and accepted into the community. They no longer hid inside the closed walls of their homes. They ventured out and began to live full lives instead of the lonely lives of the shunned.

Confirmation

Danny and I were sitting on the beach one day after life had settled down following the gala. I was studying and finishing up my long-desired medical degree. A textbook lay open on my lap, but my mind was elsewhere.

I was remembering the connections I made with Alexa in the eighth grade and with Anna when I was an aide at

Shriners Hospital. Both times I felt drawn to pediatric medicine. My heart was so touched by children and young people who experience illness or struggle with long-term medical conditions.

Now this experience with Christopher fulfilled me way beyond my expectations. People really *could* care for a kid like Christopher and accept a man like me.

"Danny," I said as I rubbed his neck behind his ears, "I see what field God wants me to enter. It's finally clear and confirmed in my heart."

Danny looked at me with his canine smile of approval.

"Let's go," I said to him as he took his place by my side. "I want to find Laura and tell her I have definitely decided to go into pediatric medicine."

Laura and I were still just friends.

I silently pondered that phrase, "just friends." *Do I dare wonder if we could ever be more?*

The answer to that question took awhile to unfold!

10

SAYING YES TO LOVE

"Well, we got a lot done," I (Laura) said after studying with Tyler for several hours at his "garage" apartment. We both stood up from the small table, and Tyler came around close to me. He hugged me, just like he usually did when I left to go back to my apartment.

But wait, I thought, as his hand slipped down from my shoulder to the small of my back. He pulled me in tighter than he usually did and held me longer.

This is definitely not the usual hug, I said to myself. *This is not the hug of one friend to another.*

I put my arms around him and with the same intensity he did. We didn't speak. We just held each other for a few moments and then leaned back and smiled at what we both understood. Our 10-month agreement to be "just friends" seemed to be moving in a different direction. We didn't really talk about what was happening. I think we were both cautious about jeopardizing the amazing friendship we enjoyed.

I know I was initially terrified of messing up our friendship. We had quickly become friends and study partners. In fact, Tyler was my *best* friend. Life and school on Statia was often challenging and lonely. Our friendship was my way of surviving.

Working together on Christopher's benefit gala only deepened our feelings of connection. Any time you work on a big, chaotic project, opportunities arise for conflicts with fellow team members. But Tyler and I worked beautifully together, seamlessly helping and supporting each other at every step along the way.

An Emotional Walk

The year was speeding by, and before we knew it, it was time for Christmas break. The two of us would now go our separate ways for a few weeks to be with family: me to Canada and Tyler to Florida.

This absence would be painful after spending so much time together. Even worse, I knew Tyler would be seeing friends back at his family's church, including some local girls he had once liked. The more I thought about Tyler potentially reconnecting with old girlfriends, the more upset I became.

I love this man! I told myself. *I can't let him go home and go on dates with other girls. It's time I let him know how I really feel.*

My emotions were already churning from an experience Tyler and I had just shared. We'd both been trained to operate the hyperbaric chamber at the hospital. This chamber is used to help scuba divers who have experienced decompression sickness as a result of coming to the surface too fast.

The lead hyperbaric medicine specialist was off the island when a diver had a terrible accident and needed to go into the chamber. Tyler and I worked with this man for 36 hours, putting him in and out of the chamber in an attempt to save his life. He survived, and he was enormously grateful for these two medical students who never gave up on him.

We met this man at the airport to say good-bye a few days later. As he walked onto the tiny plane, all smiles, Tyler and I fell into each other's arms in gratitude that he survived and overwhelmed by the bond we now shared. We had saved a life together.

I was ruminating on all of this in my apartment, which was more than two miles from Tyler's place. He would usually pick me up in his dune buggy, but I needed to talk to him *now*!

I slipped on my walking shoes and took off. I moved quickly, slowing only slightly as I ascended the steep incline students jokingly called Cardiac Hill. This particular two-and-one-half miles was no easy terrain. Finally I had reached Tyler's apartment.

"Tyler!" I yelled as I just barged in the door.

I knew he'd be lying on his bed in the back room with the bedroom door closed and air conditioner cranked up.

"Tyler! You can't go home to Florida. I think I love you!" I yelled again as I barged through that door too.

I came to a screeching halt as I saw a girl's face looking back at Tyler on his computer. He slammed the computer shut as he told his friend that he'd call her later.

"Bring it in," he said with a smile and opened his arms to pull me into a hug. He kissed me, and I relaxed for the first time in almost an hour.

We both went home to our families for Christmas break. I guessed that Tyler had already invited a friend on a date, but my confidence calmed me enough to follow through with our original visits home.

Hidden Fears

Pretty soon we were dating each other exclusively. I could tell that Tyler loved me too, but there was something holding him back from opening his heart to me. It was fear.

Nearly everyone struggles with doubts and insecurities, but in Tyler's case his doubts were confirmed by years of hard evidence. Only a relatively small percentage of his female acquaintances considered him datable material. There had been many girls who liked Tyler and talked to him, but few had been willing to venture across that invisible line between friendship and romance. I had crossed over that line, but now Tyler seemed unsure.

As I pieced things together, I could see Tyler's fear came from mistaken ideas he had about himself. He never expressed it in so many words, but his view was: *I'm okay with myself as a person, but I'm not so sure of my prospects as a romantic partner or husband.*

Tyler also had concerns about his financial prospects. He said he wouldn't get married until he could provide financially for his wife and children. Right now he was broke, knee-deep in college debt, and years away from completing his training and landing the kind of good-paying hospital position that could support a family.

But there was another fear that gripped Tyler, as I would find out one night over dinner.

It was the fall of 2009, and Tyler and I were having dinner in a Florida restaurant.

We had both finished our med school time on the island and had made plans to meet each other's families. After a few weeks at home in Canada, I had flown to Tampa to study for the first of many medical licensure exams and to become acquainted with Tyler's family. Following the exams, Tyler would fly back to Canada with me to meet my family.

The restaurant was right across the street from the Shriners Hospital in Tampa, a place where Tyler had worked with many disabled children. We had spent the day at Shriners, and I was able to walk through the halls where Tyler had been wheeled to so many surgeries as a little boy. He introduced me to his second family—all of "his girls" who had worked with him and had been instrumental in Christopher's coming to Shriners.

After ordering dinner, we talked about what a great day it had been.

"It would be so awesome if we could come back here and work," I said, picturing our future home and life together.

"Laura," Tyler said with real apprehension in his voice. "I don't know how long I can do this."

"What are you talking about?" I asked with a puzzled look on my face.

"I don't know how long it will be before I'm in a wheelchair. My body has been badly broken, and I know I may end up in a wheelchair at some point."

"I can't wait to be old people in wheelchairs running over people walking," I said, attempting humor to break the somber tone of Tyler's words.

"This is not the life for you," he said definitively.

"What?" I shot back, angry about his decisive remark. "You can't choose my life for me. I get to love whoever I want to love."

I stood up and stormed out to the car. Tyler paid the check and caught up to me. Sitting silently behind the wheel, he drove me to where I was staying in Tampa and then left. We hadn't said a word since leaving the restaurant. Later that night, I looked out the window and saw him sitting in his car in the driveway. I stepped outside and climbed into the passenger seat.

"There is one thing that scares me away from love," Tyler told me. "Being in a wheelchair and being married to you just don't fit together. Frankly, I don't really know if I could ever embrace any picture of my future that involved my wife pushing my wheelchair."

He told me about Bobbie, a good friend in fifth grade who had fun pushing Tyler around school in a wheelchair. Now he was trying to picture what it would be like to have me push him around someday, and he didn't like the looks of it.

"I'm never going to be normal," he said, circling back to his doubts about whether he was potential marriage material. He told me he saw marriage as a lifelong relationship between a prince and his princess. "The prince should care for the princess," he said, "not the other way around."

I had already thought about all this. I knew that if we were able to be together for 50 years, there was a high possibility of Tyler winding up in a wheelchair. That was something I accepted.

"Tyler, you mean you're going to throw our future together away because you're afraid of something that I've already accepted?"

"I just can't do it, Laura. I'm sorry," he said.

Going Home Alone

The next day Tyler took me to the airport and put me on a plane back to my home in Canada. Our plan had been for him to come with me, but I got on the plane alone that day.

I couldn't believe how our happiness had evaporated in 24 hours. I was miserable. I went through the days, and nights, trying to absorb what had happened. We were so good together, and he was sabotaging our relationship over something that didn't exist; I totally accepted the realities of his disability and wanted to spend my life with him no matter what the future held.

"Something will be coming in the mail."

Tyler texted me this message a few weeks after we'd broken up but gave no indication if the "something" was good news or bad news. I waited for the mystery "something" to arrive, not sure if I should be hopeful about what he was sending or dreading it.

A few days later, a package came in the mail. I ripped into it and smiled as the face of a stuffed animal stared back at me. It was actually a dog dressed in a leather jacket with a stethoscope hanging around his neck. A handwritten note was tucked into the dog's jacket. The note read, "I've loved you since the day I met you. I'm so sorry. Think about it. If you decide, I'm all in."

I immediately called him and said, "I'm *in*!"

Who's Disabled?

People asked me what I saw in Tyler, and I was always glad to tell them.

One friend asked me, "If the two of you were to get married and have children someday, does cerebral palsy put your children at risk?"

"No," I said. "Most forms of CP—including Tyler's—aren't genetic. And CP isn't communicable. It can't be spread."

When some people look at Tyler, the first and only thing they see is disability. But I never viewed him as "disabled." Don't get me wrong. I knew he had CP. But Tyler refused to be defined by it, and I didn't let CP define him either. Once we got past his faulty image of himself as a husband, his CP was just one part of a totally wonderful human being.

Our relationship developed its own quirky rhythms, like the time early on during our med school days when we went for a moonlit romantic walk on the sandy beach. Every couple needs at least one beach walk. We were living on a tropical island paradise, so why not enjoy it?

A few minutes into our picture-postcard-perfect romantic moment, Tyler stumbled over a rock in the sand and fell down. I fell to my knees in front of him, laughing out loud and giving him a big hug.

"I can't believe you laughed at me," he said, pretending to be mad. Then he cracked up and started laughing too. It was a glorious, joyous, and utterly romantic moment.

Then there was the cake escapade. We thought taking a cake to class would help break the ice with some of the other med school students. One night I baked a nice cake, covered with icing. Tyler came to pick me up for class the next morning, but as he was carrying the cake, he slipped and fell down the stairs. It was like one of those slow-motion movie scenes, with Tyler and the cake independently bouncing down the eight or nine steps to the landing.

"Oh, my goodness!" I heard Tyler say on his way down the stairs.

When the dust had settled, Tyler was bruised but not badly injured.

"Well," I said. "I guess I'm going to have to bake another cake, aren't I?"

This was just another one of those "palsy moments" that didn't faze me.

When I look at Tyler, I see a man who has refused to allow his life to be circumscribed by physical challenges. In fact, Tyler had accomplished more in his life than most of the able-bodied men I've known.

I do get upset whenever I see other people harassing or belittling Tyler. We've been to restaurants where waiters refused to serve us. We've been in movie theaters where people actually yelled, "Hey, what's the blind guy doing in a movie?"

I'm his advocate in these situations, but I need to watch what I say so I don't lose my temper at people over the way they treat Tyler.

The Measure of a Man

There's so much good that I see in Tyler. For one thing, I admire his integrity. He tells the truth and does what he says he will do. He is a man of strong character.

Tyler's love for children and animals drew me right in as I saw him relate to the island children and, of course, to his dog, Danny. Apparently some of the islanders could see how much Tyler loved animals, because one day they gave us a call. A litter of eight-week-old puppies had been abandoned at a local garbage dump. Could we help save them? We agreed to find the puppies. Tyler got down on the ground and crawled through piles of garbage to rescue the pups, enjoying the whole experience.

Tyler's deep faith was clearly apparent in the way he lived his life. I had become skeptical about Christianity because of the hypocrisy I'd witnessed over the years. It seemed that many Christians believed one thing but did something else. They preached about loving others but were then unkind. I had not been raised in any formal belief system. Instead, I was encouraged to find my own philosophy as I made my way through life.

Tyler challenged my experience with Christianity. He's no hypocrite about his faith. He has integrity as a man and as a believer. I was not a Christian when we met, so it was fascinating to be with someone who truly walked the walk and sought to live his life in a way that was consistent with biblical teaching. He made me look at faith in an entirely new way. For the first time I understood what people meant when they talked about having a "personal relationship with Jesus."

Faith in God was a huge part of Tyler's life, but it was virtually absent in mine. I was concerned my skeptical background could cause problems, but he never pressured me about religion, so I didn't worry about it, either. His faith actually challenged me to think more intentionally about my own values and beliefs.

One evening I decided to reach out to God and see if He would reach back to me.

"Jesus, I've heard that You loved the world so much that You died for us. If that's true, and if You are there, and if You love me, please give me some kind of sign."

I don't know what I was expecting.

What actually happened next was even more amazing. Lying there in my bed, I suddenly experienced a strange sensation, a slight pressure in my chest. Then I realized it was Jesus hugging my heart by giving it a tiny little squeeze. This brief hug was an expression of love directly from God to me, and I wholeheartedly embraced it.

"Jesus, please accept me as I am," I said.

No angel sang. No trumpets blew. But my heart remained strangely warmed. Somehow I knew something important had happened to me that night.

Doctors in Love

When I told Tyler I was *in*, our commitment to each other quickly grew.

We would have gladly rushed directly to the local justice of the peace for an immediate wedding, but there was a problem. Both of us still had long roads to travel in our studies and training. We knew that, at times, those roads would diverge and require us to go in separate directions for months at a time to pursue our varied training.

There remained many additional hoops for both of us to jump through before we could become husband and wife.

Mission Accomplished

After all of our educational work was completed and our residencies were finished, Tyler and I secured several professional acronyms that communicate our achievements to the world. I've earned three sets of acronyms:

- MD: Doctor of Medicine with a graduate degree from a medical school.
- FAAP: Fellow of the American Academy of Pediatrics. This means I'm a specialist in pediatric medicine.
- FCCM: Fellow of Critical Care Medicine, providing care for children who are critically ill. Some of these children are dealing with the most extreme diseases. I am able to work in critical care facilities and provide care for some of the most extreme diseases.

Tyler has the MD along with a few additional acronyms after his name. Three of the acronyms are connected to hyperbaric wound treatment:

- CHWS: Certified Hyperbaric Wound Specialist.
- CHT: Certified Hyperbaric Technologist. Certified Hand Therapist. These specialists help people restore function to their upper extremities.
- CHS: Certified Hyperbaric Specialist. That means Tyler can manage and operate a hyperbaric chamber for healing difficult wounds.
- MAPWCA: Master within the American Professional Wound Care Association. "Master" means Tyler is considered a key opinion leader in the field.
- DMT: Diver Medic Technician. People with these letters after their names are the emergency medical technicians of the underwater and scuba-diving world.

Together at Last

We spent so much time acquiring the acronyms *after* our names that we didn't have time to get the Mr. and Mrs. *before* our names until October 7, 2012.

We were married in Safety Harbor, Florida, because so many people in Tyler's church community and so many medical professionals in that area had supported him and his family through all his growing-up years. They had poured so much prayer and love into Tyler accomplishing his dream of becoming a doctor, and now this special young man was getting married. Our celebration would have been incomplete without them.

My Canadian family and friends were also thrilled to join us at our outdoor ceremony. We said our wedding vows under the canopy of a beautiful shade-giving tree. Danny was our best man, and I'd given him a handsome white leash as his formal attire.

As I walked down the aisle on the arm of my father, Tyler and Danny stood up front looking elegant and happy. A contented thought flashed across my mind as I remembered how hard it had been to win over Danny. He was trained to protect Tyler from everything and everyone, including me. There were so many times when Danny would sit or stand between Tyler and me that I thought we'd never be able to be right next to each other. Danny finally realized that I was part of their lives for the long haul. He knew he could trust me around Tyler, and Danny and I grew to love each other. Being accepted by Danny was like getting the seal of approval from Tyler's best friend. That friend may have been a canine, but he was as important as any human friend would have been.

Long-Distance Life

Getting married didn't mean we would be living full-time in the same house with each other. Different job locations meant we lived in different cities for some of our marriage, but it worked for us. We each have such a deep understanding about the demands of our medical work that we're able to adjust to some of the unconventional ways we live to make our marriage work.

It wasn't until June of 2018—more than five years after our marriage—that we moved into our own home together. We still work in two different places: I work in Jackson, Mississippi, more than three hours from Tyler's work in Pascagoula, Mississippi. Our home is in Pascagoula. I maintain a 12-day shift in Jackson, which lets me be home the rest of each month. It's so wonderful for the two of us to be able to "go home" and have that mean we're going to the same house.

We share that home with our five youngsters: our beautiful three-year-old daughter, Harper Grace, my three dogs, and Tyler's service dog.

Was it all worth the 13 years of studying and training, as well as the time apart? We believe so. There's so much we want to do as we serve together. We're not sure what the future holds, but it looks bright.

11

THE GREAT PHYSICIAN

Walking into Singing River Hospital in Pascagoula, Mississippi, I (Tyler) smile at the volunteers manning the welcome desk. I wonder if those nice ladies know what goes through my mind as I enter this place?

Could they even guess how I feel returning every day to a setting where I spent so much of my childhood? Not that I had all those surgeries in this particular hospital. No, not here, where I'm known as Dr. Tyler Sexton. Still, those other hospitals where I spent so much time as a patient have much in common with this hospital. Except I'm no longer the patient. In this hospital, I'm the chair of pediatrics.

So how do I feel when I walk through the hospital's doors?

Humble. I feel humble. Humility fills my mind and my heart, and I hope it shows in my attitude toward every person I meet each day I enter here.

In living out my calling as a doctor, I try to follow in the footsteps of Jesus, whose work healing bodies, minds, and spirits has led many to call Him the Great Physician. Mark's Gospel tells the fascinating story of Christ healing both the body and spirit of the paralyzed man who was lowered from the roof into a crowded room in Capernaum.

"Son, your sins are forgiven," Jesus told the man. That upset teachers of the law, who accused Jesus of blasphemy for claiming that He could forgive sins. But in order to prove that His claim was true, Jesus followed up by healing the man and commanding him to walk. Jesus healed the man's spirit when He forgave his sins, and He healed the man's body when He removed the paralysis.

St. Augustine, the fifth-century bishop and theologian, said that Christ is "that Physician who heals our inward sight and enables us to behold that very light eternal which is himself."[1]

I try to emulate the Great Physician as best I can every time I report to work, as I attempt to care for people's spirits and minds as well as their bodies. For me, being a servant of the Great Physician means that when I see patients hurting, I hurt deep down with them. Sometimes I cry with them, just as Jesus wept about the death of His good friend Lazarus. Sometimes I pray with them when they ask me to.

As a disciple of the Great Physician, I look for opportunities to serve in unexpected and sometimes desperate scenarios where both my patients and I can be surprised by what God does in our midst. Come along with me on a typical day at Singing River so you can see how Christ shows up in some amazing ways.

Superheroes

After I walk through the doors at Singing River, I don't put on a white coat like many doctors do. White coats can affect patients—and not in a good way. Patients may start to feel anxious about what the man or woman in the white coat will do to them or tell them. There's even a phrase to describe this reaction: "white coat syndrome." The technical name is "white coat hypertension" because people who respond this way exhibit a higher than normal blood pressure.

My "uniform" is a sports jacket over a superhero T-shirt. I like my wardrobe to show off fictional icons like Batman, Superman, and The Flash because the kids I meet here are my superheroes. I look at these children with whatever is broken in them, and I see great value. They have value just as they are. They may need a cure for a disease or a treatment to improve a disability, or even years of surgeries to be able to walk and realize their childhood dreams. But they are created in the image of God and are wonderful without changing a thing.

Every day my second service dog named Danny and I take the elevator up to the third floor. My superhero persona is highlighted in my office by a bat symbol illuminated on the ceiling. As Danny and I walk through the hospital halls on the way to a patient's room, people line up to see my dog. We're the Dynamic Duo cruising along. When we approach kids in wheelchairs, I let Danny put his head close to them and sniff them in a soft and loving way.

When I show up in a patient's room, I often see surprised looks and questioning expressions on the faces of the parents. I smile broadly and greet them and their child. Then they notice that the stethoscope around my neck is covered with a Batman sheath and my T-shirt sports some other superhero character. Those details communicate to my patients and their parents that I'm someone who knows and loves children. Their discomfort with my strange walk and wandering eyes diminishes quickly, and they become more comfortable with me.

But the greater comfort, especially for the kids, is Danny. It's amazing how sick kids and worried parents react when they see him. Unless they are committed dog dislikers, they *ooh* and *ahhh*, and my disabilities seem to disappear completely.

And when we walk into the room of a child with special needs, the parents and kids all seem to relax a little. My disability gives me credibility. Danny wags his tail and sits patiently while I talk to the parents and the child. When I'm done I take his harness off and tell the kids they can pet him because he's no longer working. Without the harness, Danny knows he can be engaged with others and show them some puppy love—even though he isn't a puppy anymore.

The kids love Danny *and* my shirts. In addition to making kids more comfortable with their doctor, my wardrobe gives me the chance to encourage them to wage a superhuman fight for their healthy recovery. I like talking to my patients about my favorite fictional hero—Barry Allen (a.k.a. The Flash)—a normal human who was struck by lightning one day and gained the super power of excessive speed, which he uses along with his speedy intellect to fight evil and do good.

Every once in a while I have the opportunity to serve families who have just welcomed a new baby into the world with CP.

"Your son has been diagnosed with cerebral palsy," I told one mother and father. "That's what I have. And we're going to work on this together. Your son is worth it, and we're going to take this step by step."

Some doctors won't see certain patients because they have "special needs." Those children may never function with complete wellness, but their value is as priceless as the more accomplished among us. I try to see each patient with the loving depth of Jesus. He is my model.

Jesus saw me that way when I was born with an incurable condition. If I had never learned to walk or achieved academically, His deep love and total acceptance would still have blessed me. And I want to bless the children I care for at the hospital.

They come to me at their worst times, and I tell them

their wounds are beautiful. "I'll be by your side and help those wounds to heal," I tell them.

I give these children messages I've learned from my life with a broken body and a faithful God:

> You're strong and brave, even when you're sad and are crying. Being strong and brave isn't about pretending that nothing hurts. Being strong and brave is about being yourself as God created you to be. And do you know what? He wants you to be as well as possible. I trusted God when I was a little boy in a hospital, just like you, and He helped me to become a doctor so I can now help you.

The T-shirts and talk of superheroes are creative touches that help make the work fun, both for me and for my patients. But at the same time, I never forget that hospitals can be sad and terrifying places for so many people. Most people don't welcome opportunities to go to hospitals, which can be full of pain, misery, and even death. But I see hospitals as great places to practice healing, encouragement, and the restoration of both bodies and souls.

Invisible Service

I was driving to the home of new parents, knowing this visit would be one of those terribly sad times when I could not be who they hoped I would be.

Their infant son had been born two days earlier with numerous life-threatening complications. The medical staff and I quickly realized that this little one would probably only survive a few days, so the parents took their newborn home to spend his remaining time with them in the comfort of his beautiful nursery.

This couple still hoped the diagnosis was wrong, and that Dr. Sexton would arrive with good news. A doctor they trust can create optimism just with his or her presence. I could tell by the look in their eyes that they longed for me to work some kind of miracle to bring their baby boy to good health. But I couldn't do that.

I knew when I looked at their tiny son, quiet in his mother's arms, that he was almost gone. Within minutes I uttered words no parent wants to hear.

"He's gone. I'm so very sorry," I whispered as I looked into the eyes of these grieving parents.

In these situations, there's nothing else to say. Being present, with tears and touch and silence, is all anyone can do in those solemn moments of inexplicable loss.

I didn't visit those parents because it was part of my job. I don't think I even mentioned these visits to the staff at the hospital. My only goal is to be present and ready to respond whenever God nudges me to walk alongside people in moments of darkest sorrow.

Sometimes I feel God is most pleased with me when, unbeknownst to anyone else in the world, I love and care for people who are utterly unable to do anything for me in return. It's during these times of nearly invisible service that I feel I'm pursuing my calling and following most closely in the footsteps of the Great Physician.

Sometimes the darkness seems especially strong, but when that's the case there are amazing opportunities for the light to shine through. I took care of one young girl who had been sexually abused in a horrific way. I also cared for an 11-year-old girl who had been forced into prostitution and given birth to her baby in an empty field. I never know if these patients experience any of the love and compassion I'm investing in them, but I believe that caring for people's broken hearts can be as important as healing their broken bodies. Hopefully, the light of God's love will touch them with a word I say to communicate loving care.

I could avoid some of these harrowing cases if I wanted to, but I welcome them. I hate the reality that any of these abuses happen at all, but I am eager to offer safety, acceptance, and loving care.

These children and young people suffer trauma unlike many of us will ever know. Their need for love is desperate. While it's personally difficult to witness the results of such terrible abuse, it's also an affirmation that I'm doing what Jesus would do. He would draw near to them and begin a process of deep healing. I'm not Jesus, so my care may not bring positive results to these patients. But if I didn't try to help them, I'd be turning away from my calling to follow the Great Physician.

Sometimes I help patients who have been referred to the

hospital by the Human Services departments of local counties. I may be called to give testimony in court about the physical results of the abuse. Some doctors don't want to take these cases because they involve more work and participating in an unpleasant process. I do this willingly because these innocent children need advocates to give voice to the darkness of the things done to them.

It's difficult to understand how one human can hurt another human with such terrible cruelty. It's especially disturbing when so many cases involve parents harming their own child.

I think of my daughter, Harper Grace, and I see the way she looks at me with total trust and unconditional love. How could I *ever* do anything to harm her? In her eyes I see myself as her hero, her protector.

If only an abusive father or mother could see themselves as their child sees them, maybe they could stop abuse before it starts.

I know this is a complicated issue with no easy solution. I try to do what I can to help the wounded bodies and souls I see, and then I go to my heavenly Father to restore my own soul.

We are taught as doctors to not become personally involved with our patients. It's true that we must not let our emotions impair our judgment concerning the best treatment for anyone, but I do open my heart to the pain of my patients.

That openness allows pain to touch me, so I need to

acknowledge my feelings and spend time with the Great Physician for my own healing. It's truly a blessing to give emotional support, and it's also a blessing to receive it from my Father.

Amazed

Now you know a little about what my days as a practicing pediatrician entail. There are good and sad times, victories and seeming defeats. Those seeming defeats happen when I'm unable to help a child the way I would hope I could. My life is an example of what *seemed* to be a medical defeat when doctors said I would never walk. But with numerous surgeries and procedures and the faith of my parents, I am walking. I have a full life. I am blessed. What may seem like a defeat turned into a victory.

Death certainly seems like a defeat, but Jesus overcame death. Death results in terrible loss and pain, but our promise of eternal life if we accept Jesus as our Lord and Savior turns that pain and loss into ultimate victory.

Along with my work as a pediatrician, I've also been pleased to be a part of Focus on the Family's Physicians Resource Council. This council was founded in 1987, and today it advises Focus on some of the more complicated moral and ethical issues in modern medicine.

Looking back, I'm still amazed that I made it here at all. Part of the humbling process I experienced was how people with disabilities are often judged inaccurately. I really did believe that God had called me to follow the Great Physician, but I wasn't sure I would ever get the opportunity to put my skill into practice.

Apparently I'm not the only disabled person to face this obstacle. You may be surprised, but many medical professionals harbor doubts about the abilities of disabled people. This dilemma is explored in ABC's popular TV show *The Good Doctor*.

As I mentioned earlier, Dr. Shaun Murphy, the show's central character, is a gifted surgeon who has a mild form of autism. He was hired only because one of the hospital administrators, a character named Aaron Glassman, knew him well and lobbied to hire him, against the strenuous opposition of some of the other doctors:

"We hire Shaun, and we give hope to those people who have limitations that those limitations are not what they think they are, that they do have a shot," said Glassman in the pilot episode of the show. "We hire Shaun, and we make this hospital better for it. We hire Shaun, and we are better people for it."[2]

I prayed that God would guide me to someone who might be brave and stubborn enough to hire me, even though I did have CP. God answered that prayer more powerfully than I ever could have imagined.

Let me introduce you to my boss, Dr. Randy Roth, the Chief Medical Officer of the Singing River Health System in Pascagoula, Mississippi.

The "It" Factor

I (Dr. Randy Roth) became aware of Tyler Sexton when we had a staffing shortage in our pediatric department. I received a phone call from a hospital in Mobile, Alabama, recommending Tyler Sexton, a first-year resident there. We decided to interview him and see if he would fit in our department. I didn't know anything about Tyler having disability issues.

I set up an initial meeting at a local steakhouse and got there early to prepare. A short while later, I saw a man walk in accompanied by his wife and a service dog.

That can't be Dr. Tyler Sexton! I remember telling myself. I was wrong, and I was worried about what I saw.

In the time it took Tyler to get from the entrance to my table, three major questions went through my mind:

1. Can a man with this condition handle the hard physical labor required of him as a doctor working long shifts?
2. What will patients think if a doctor who has his own physical challenges treats them? I could just imagine hearing one of the locals saying, *Hey, this guy can't even walk well by himself. How can he take care of my child?*
3. Am I willing to risk making a costly professional blunder on my first really big hiring decision? This was perhaps the biggest question going through my mind.

> *Is it really worth risking my career to hire this man?* At the time, I was relatively new in my position as the Singing River Hospital's Chief Medical Officer. As the CMO, I'm responsible for hiring and supervising all the doctors on our staff.

But as soon as I said hello to Tyler and began talking with him, these fears receded. Within about five minutes of Tyler sitting down and saying hello to me, I was totally at ease with him and his disability.

When you're hiring someone, there's more to consider than technical competence. Yes, you want someone who can do the job, but you want more. I quickly realized that Tyler was very special and possessed something that I call the "it" factor.

The "it" factor can be hard to discern, but some doctors clearly have it, while others do not. Physicians who have this special quality can walk into a hospital room full of sick, sad, upset people and immediately instill confidence among not only the patients but all their friends and family members. Doctors who possess this ability can instantly transform fearful strangers into devoted allies who believe in them and trust them. Tyler's got the "it" factor in spades, as his work here at the hospital has clearly shown.

Five years after hiring Tyler, it's now clear that this was one of the better decisions of my career. In a short time, he persuasively answered each of the three questions that had disturbed me when I first met him.

As for the first question, Tyler can handle the work, and he never says no when asked to do something more. If anything, we have to throttle him back.

Early on, one doctor was disparaging about my decision, telling me, "I can't believe that you hired this guy." But within a week of arriving here, Tyler performed a difficult, hours-long C-section delivery, putting to rest any questions about his strength and stamina.

As for the second question, patients are completely accepting of Tyler just as he is, particularly the kids, who love his dog and his superhero T-shirts. The kids Tyler takes care of immediately feel at ease with him, and the whole superhero thing captures their imaginations. Patients and their parents love both Tyler and Danny.

We had never had a service dog in our staff areas before, and I was worried that some patients might complain. I'd had years of experience hearing people complain about how bad the hospital food tastes, how hot or how cold the rooms are, how the TV is not working, how they waited for hours in the emergency room, or how when they finally got to see a doctor he was rude to them. But I haven't received a single complaint about Danny, who often does double duty as a therapy pet.

When you see Tyler at work, it doesn't take long to realize that he's a toucher. He sits down next to kids, holds their hands, and tells them, "Look, I've been through things like this before, and I think you're going to come out all right."

Patients put a lot of trust and faith in a doctor who takes care of them like that. As one child told me, "Having a broken doctor makes me feel better."

As for question number three, my decision to hire Tyler has led a few people to believe that I am some kind of brilliant CMO. But I'm no genius. It's just that Tyler has brought a dynamic to our organization that we didn't have before. His mission is to make the place where he works a better place for everybody. He has been a bonanza for us.

Tyler is always looking to do more and to help more people, and he has enthusiastically embraced opportunities to be the hospital's roving ambassador to local communities, speaking at schools, churches, and civic events about disabilities, mental health, and other issues people care about.

My six kids attend a Catholic school where Tyler was invited to speak about bullying. He spoke so honestly and passionately about being bullied because of his disability that kids at the school are still talking about Tyler. His talk motivated some students to be more vigilant in watching for and reporting instances of school bullying.

I knew early on that Tyler had the "it" factor, but at the time I didn't realize I was hiring a doctor with the ability to walk into a room of 700 students and quickly convince them to quiet down and listen to him.

As a result of these activities, Tyler has become something of a local celebrity. Thanks to stories in the local newspaper and on local TV news shows, people bring their kids to our hospital for care and tell us, "We want the doctor with the dog!"

When Tyler became a national celebrity through his appearance on ABC's *20/20*, the local media provided even more wonderful coverage. Tyler was one of a number of doctors from around the country who told their stories in a special edition of *20/20* that introduced the first episode of *The Good Doctor*.

Tyler talked about his disability as well as his faith in God. Some hospitals might frown on physicians talking about faith, but that's not a big issue here in coastal Mississippi, where nearly 80 percent of the population say they are Baptists. Religion is a huge part of people's lifestyles here. I'm a Catholic who speaks freely about my own religion with my patients when appropriate.

Tyler and I come from different Christian traditions, but we share the belief that the God who created all of us is a loving God and that Christ is a healer, the Great Physician.

A doctor never wants to press his personal beliefs on his patients, but when patients themselves pray, or when they request you to pray with them or for them, it seems as if that should be part of our mission as healers.

I wouldn't recommend that every doctor try to pray with patients. People here in Mississippi can see right through someone who doesn't have his heart in it. But patients can see that Tyler walks humbly with God, and that really helps when they are scared.

From Geek to Cool

After I (Tyler) appeared on the *20/20* TV show, I was suddenly valued as a cool guy. Instead of being the doctor who walked funny and wore silly T-shirts, I was the "guy on that TV show."

The people at *20/20* did their best to slather makeup all over my balding head and the bags under my eyes. I'd been doing some public speaking by the time the filming happened, so I wasn't nervous, but I was excited and grateful to have the opportunity to be part of such an important topic. It was an opportunity for viewers of the show to look at people with disabilities as capable of overcoming obstacles and entering the professional career market.

On a personal level, it's certainly more fun to be cool instead of geeky! Kids love having a celebrity doctor take care of them, particularly if the doctor has his very own Facebook page.

"We're so glad it's you," parents sometimes tell me even though I'm the same guy I was before I enjoyed this sudden celebrity.

The true celebrity—and the true superhero—is of course the Great Physician, who loved me and helped through all of the surgeries and suffering, through the bullying and rejection, through the lonely years and difficulties of med school, and through each and every obstacle on the way to fulfilling the calling He gave me.

Yes, when I walk through the doors every day at Singing River Hospital, I'm humbled to be the servant of the Great Physician, the ultimate healer of bodies and souls.

12

YES, YOU *CAN*

So to keep me from becoming conceited because of the surpassing greatness of the revelations, a thorn was given me in the flesh, a messenger of Satan to harass me, to keep me from becoming conceited. Three times I pleaded with the Lord about this, that it should leave me. But he said to me, "My grace is sufficient for you, for my power is made perfect in weakness." Therefore I will boast all the more gladly of my weaknesses, so that the power of Christ may rest upon me. For the sake of Christ, then, I am content with weaknesses, insults, hardships, persecutions, and calamities. For when I am weak, then I am strong.

2 CORINTHIANS 12:7-10

The apostle Paul wrote these words in his letter to the church at Corinth. Like Paul, I (Tyler) have asked God a number of times in the past to remove the "thorn" of cerebral palsy from my body. God has said, "No." So you can understand why Paul's message is my life verse.

Scholars have debated for centuries whether this was some kind of physical problem, like difficulties with his eyesight, or a psychological or emotional problem like depression. But what the specific thorn was is not the point. The point is Paul's response to the thorn.

Did Paul complain to God about his trials and tribulations? Did he resign his apostolic calling and ask for an easier assignment?

No, Paul did something that many other people don't do. He accepted the pain and embraced the suffering as part and parcel of human life, saying, "Not only that, but we rejoice in our sufferings, knowing that suffering produces endurance, and endurance produces character, and character produces hope, and hope does not put us to shame, because God's love has been poured into our hearts through the Holy Spirit who has been given to us" (Romans 5:3-5).

Godly Influences

I was born with cerebral palsy but not with automatic acceptance of this thorn in my flesh. You've just read my story, so you know that I started life with struggles that continued for many years. Most of the time I held on to the teaching and life-view of my godly parents, but being a little boy who was picked on and bullied a lot, I had my fair share of times when I cried out to God, "Why me?"

Blessedly, those times didn't last long. My mom was so diligent in talking to me about how God created me and loved me just as I am, and my dad always believed that God would grant their prayer that I would walk one day. They didn't preach or press me to hide my feelings. It was okay to be upset or disappointed or angry. And when those painful emotions settled down, my parents were the first to point me back to my heavenly Father.

Being a Christian wasn't about a long list of things we should or should not do. It was about trusting that God loved us and had our best interests in His plan for our lives. God used my parents to touch my own heart. By the time I was in middle school, I knew that God had a plan for me that included many blessings along with having CP. I knew He loved me. I just flat-out believed Him.

I gladly told others about Jesus, and I also shared how doctors might say I would never walk, but Jesus gave us hope that I would.

Joy in Suffering

I often talk to people about experiencing life with joy in the midst of suffering. Some seem to understand me right away. Others give me quizzical looks. They think "joy in suffering" is some kind of oxymoron.

Joy in suffering is the story of my life. It also happens to be a major theme in the Bible, though some people don't seem to realize that.

Over the years I've heard hundreds of messages claiming, "God wants you to be healthy and wealthy. Just name it and claim it, and send in a generous donation, and you can live pain-free."

When some people hear enough of these kinds of sermons, they reach the curious conclusion that the Christian life is supposed to be an uninterrupted series of miracles and victories.

But if following God is supposed to lead to a pain-free life, someone forgot to tell Jesus, who was crucified for our salvation. And someone forgot to tell Paul, whose letters to the early churches overflow with descriptions of pains, trials, and tribulations.

After Jesus, the apostle Paul is my favorite hero of the faith. He certainly didn't have an easy life, as he testified to the church at Corinth.

> Are they servants of Christ? I am a better one—I am talking like a madman—with far greater labors, far more imprisonments, with countless beatings, and often near death. Five times I received at the hands of the Jews the forty lashes less one. Three times I was beaten with rods. Once I was stoned. Three times I was shipwrecked; a night and a day I was adrift at sea; on frequent journeys, in danger from rivers, danger from robbers, danger from my own

> people, danger from Gentiles, danger in the city, danger in the wilderness, danger at sea, danger from false brothers; in toil and hardship, through many a sleepless night, in hunger and thirst, often without food, in cold and exposure.
>
> 2 CORINTHIANS 11:23-27

And yet, this is the man who claimed God's word to him: "My grace is sufficient for you, for my power is made perfect in weakness" (2 Corinthians 12:9).

Paul accepted pain and difficulties as part of how God had poured out his love and transformed Paul's life from within.

People sometimes say things to me like this: "Tyler, you've done an awful lot in your life. Just think of how much more you could have done if you had not had a disability."

I understand the sentiment but reject the conclusion. When asked what I would choose if I could do it all over again and live life without cerebral palsy, I sometimes shock people with my answer.

"I don't want a do-over," I tell them. "I embrace life with CP. My life is richer because of it."

A Platform from God

I have the opportunity to speak in front of large audiences. Sometimes I'm standing on a stage. Stages can be dangerous, but it's not because I fear falling off into the first few rows of listeners.

No, stages are hazardous because they can become breeding grounds for pride. Lights are bright; the crowd applauds before I even say one word. The praise of the person introducing me can swell my opinion of myself. The microphone amplifies my voice to reach every eager person in the room. All eyes are on me . . . and Danny.

Danger! I'm subject to the seductive pull toward self-aggrandizement. The Bible calls that pride. I know better than to yield to that temptation.

I am weak. Anything positive or redemptive that results from my words is not because of me. It is from the power of the God I serve. Instead of seeing myself standing on a well-constructed stage, I see myself on a platform of opportunity given to me by God. His work in my life has given me name recognition that draws others to listen to what I say.

I'm humbled every time I step in front of people gathered to hear me. I guard against looking out over a crowd and claiming their applause for myself. God has given me the opportunity to speak and to write a book, but any goodness from it is from God.

On my own, I would have drowned in darkness and despair. It's all because of Jesus Christ that I say or write one word of victory. My suffering would have overwhelmed me without my relationship with Jesus. The joy from that relationship is difficult to put into words. But it's real. It's powerful. I'm blessed by seeing others who suffer receive relief and comfort when they hear about Jesus and His love for them. It's a privilege to share my own struggles.

Sweetly Broken

I (Lisa) am sitting in my chair. I turn on the lamp. I put my coffee on the table. I hold my Bible in my hand. This is my space, sitting at the feet of Jesus.

I'm sometimes emotionally and psychologically broken when I curl into myself in this sacred corner of my house. My feelings overwhelm me, and my thinking is stuck in anxiousness over one thing or another.

In this sweetly broken posture, I close my eyes, breathe deeply, and replace my anxious thoughts with the image of Jesus holding me. I literally feel like a daughter in His arms. I tell Him my heartaches, thank Him for His love and kindness, and praise Him for being the God who comes to His children personally. I feel so undeserving, yet I experience His unconditional acceptance of me.

Those moments are what get me through the tough times in my life. I arrive broken, and Jesus sweetly touches the deepest part of my soul. The tension in my body releases as I unwind my arms from clutching myself. My closed fists relax and open, resting in my lap. I pick up my Bible and read, and then I just quietly listen. An audible voice does not speak, but I spiritually sense the presence of God. Sometimes I perceive a specific word, and sometimes there is silence.

This isn't a magic spell or mind manipulation. It's a spiritual reality of living in a personal relationship with Jesus Christ. A power unlike muscle strength fills me with joy. The following verse describes it well: "You make known to me the path of life; in your presence there is fullness of joy; at your right hand are pleasures forevermore" (Psalm 16:11).

Deep Understanding

In my younger years I would pick up a phone to call a friend as soon as I felt the wash of painful emotions. Many of us do that. I would spill my hurt and then wait for words of comfort and help.

Now I am much less likely to pick up that phone—or email or text someone— before I go to the One who understands me better than I even understand myself. Psalm 139:1-6 describes God's deep knowledge of our innermost being:

> O Lord, you have searched me and known me!
> You know when I sit down and when I rise up;
>   you discern my thoughts from afar.
> You search out my path and my lying down
>   and are acquainted with all my ways.
> Even before a word is on my tongue,
>   behold, O Lord, you know it altogether.
> You hem me in, behind and before,
>   and lay your hand upon me.
> Such knowledge is too wonderful for me;
>   it is high; I cannot attain it.

Of course, God uses friends and faith communities to walk through tough times with us. But in the past, I would sometimes miss the best counsel by running to the quickest word of comfort I could find. I've learned that skipping my time at the feet of Jesus because I'm seeking reassurance from others can lead to neglecting to go to the Lord at all. Sure, we feel better after talking to someone. But then we often return to our to-do list and tell God we'll meet with Him later. The immediate hurt is slightly relieved, so our need seems lessened. But we fool ourselves. The pain will resurface unhealed.

I know now that the greatest comfort and best advice I can receive is from the One who knows me best. When I am so broken that nothing and no one can help, Jesus can. He never tells me that He can't help me!

I go to Him first and learn to accept myself just as I am, broken or not.

The Value of Scars

I don't have visible scars, but remembering Tyler's scars from multiple surgeries and falls helps me appreciate the truth they represent: They are a testimony to where he has been and how God has moved in and through his life. When he was little and I'd give him a bath, I'd see the scars and remember all he had overcome. I'd remember the pain but also the healing that brought him step by step closer to walking.

Then there are the internal scars that none of us see. For me, they are the emotional and psychological ones you've read about in this book. Those scars lived in me as open wounds for a long, long time, culminating in my attempted suicide. God used Pastor Bill to teach me to learn to tell the truth from a lie by going to God's Word and spending time with Jesus. The healing process took time, and I stumbled a lot. I would slip back into believing a lie about myself. A wound would be pricked and bleed, and the process would begin again.

Now those wounds have become scars of remembrance. I was utterly and completely broken. I did not believe I could recover, but I allowed myself to accept the help that led to wholeness.

When I remember that horrible time and the wounds that led to it, those wounds no longer are open and bleeding. They are my testimony to what God has done in my life. I fill my life with truth. The time I spend with Jesus, reading His Word and praying, heals and restores me every day.

Trust God with Your Mess

Trying to understand why something happens is a natural reaction, but I don't waste too much energy on that mental game. Instead, I focus on the one thing I know I can control: my heart. I guide my heart toward God, seeking His words of comfort, wisdom, and guidance in my life, no matter what's going on in me and around me. I go to my chair and sit at the feet of Jesus. I do what Hebrews 4:16 advises: "Let us then with confidence draw near to the throne of grace, that we may receive mercy and find grace to help in time of need."

Life is messy and often difficult. You can't change that.

What you *can* change is how you handle life's messiness and brokenness.

Every time we are broken we face a choice: Will we remain broken and allow lies to rule our lives? Or will we walk through the brokenness to a place of true healing, allowing God's love and power to flow into our brokenness, heal us, and empower us? We can trust God and say:

I *can* be forgiven.

I *can* experience healing.

I *can* accept God's love.

I *can* receive God's power into my life.

I can't always understand why things happen as they do, but I *can* choose to walk in the will of God. If I'm living in His will, I *can* experience joy in suffering, no matter what the circumstances may be.

I experienced much brokenness when Tyler was born and exhibited the problems that would ultimately be diagnosed as cerebral palsy.

But looking back on all that now, I can agree with Tyler that I would not have chosen any other way. I certainly wouldn't want to repeat the whole ordeal, but I'm grateful to see how God's love and grace have been poured into my life throughout the last 30-some years.

A Word for You

I don't know your story. Maybe you identify with my words about my relationship with Jesus because you enjoy that bond too. Maybe you have a relationship with Jesus, but you haven't grown close enough to Him to feel totally loved and understood. Or maybe you don't know or believe in Jesus at all.

Wherever you are in your spiritual journey, you matter to God. My prayer for you is for the God who loves you to send someone across your path who can speak spiritual truth into your life. That may be a friend, a minister, a speaker in a podcast, or a counselor.

You may need medical or psychological help, and I encourage you to be open to those resources. Don't wait to be as desperate as I had become. Get the professional help you need right now. Focus on the Family's counseling service offers a one-time complimentary consultation and referrals (call 1-855-771-4357 weekdays 6 a.m. to 8 p.m. Mountain Time).

If I could change one part of my story, I would have turned to the Lord much sooner. As I was slipping into serious depression, I would have asked for godly help. I was too ashamed to admit my weaknesses. I had known the Lord for a long time and told myself I should have known better. I needed someone to tell me: "You *can* get through this, and I will help you."

Maybe you feel that you are beyond being forgiven for something. We are all broken and need forgiveness. Nothing you have done can keep God's love from you.

I pray that our story has touched you and given you hope.

You *Can*, With God's Help

As you've seen, I (Tyler) have faced some formidable obstacles in my life on the way to fulfilling the dream God gave me, including my discouraging life circumstances and the words of those who thought it was impossible for me to become a doctor.

On my own, without God, "can't" might have been the dominating word in my vocabulary and the driving principle in my life. But I was never left on my own. In my earliest memories, God was with me. My belief in Him and faith in His Word has blessed me all of my life.

You've read of the hurdles that might have caused me to turn another way and give up. The bullying, the name-calling, the rejections from doctors who told me I could not be one of them—all of these challenges were terribly painful and persistent. Throughout that process, I didn't know if I would become a doctor or not. Sometimes it was so difficult to keep hanging on that letting go of my dream looked tempting.

Yet God's call on my life kept me tethered to Him.

He has a call on your life too. You may be blinded to that truth, but you *can* experience the love, joy, acceptance, hope, and joy that my mom and I have written about in these pages.

All you have to do is ask: Ask God to help you. Just call out to Him. You may be saying to yourself, *Easy for you to say, Tyler. You were an innocent child who didn't do anything wrong to have the challenges you had. But me! You don't know all the things I've done!*

No, I don't. But God does. Life isn't a contest. God helps any and all who want a relationship with Him through His Son. Your life may seem like a bunch of broken pieces to you, unable to be put back together. It's true that on your own, you can't be who you were created to be.

Step back and open your heart to the mosaic that is your life. Move away from looking closely at each tiny mistake or broken dream. Expand your vision and give room to embrace the possibilities that God wants to bring into your life. Reclaim lost hopes. Throw out lies about yourself and learn the truth of what it means to be a son or daughter of your Creator.

Yes, you will still suffer and face disappointments. That's all part of the mosaic. Yet you can experience life with God by your side and His Holy Spirit within you, no matter what you face. You *can* handle obstacles and difficulties, confident in the fact that God will always be with you, offering you His love, hope, and power, and knowing that God sees the mosaic of your life as a beautiful masterpiece.

Acknowledgments

From Lisa Sexton

Tyler: You are and always will be my darling little man. You have taught me how to have joy and praise God in all the simple things, and I love you, Bud.

My husband, Kevin: You are the love of my life. We've had so many ups and downs, but I'm so thankful that by the grace of God we hung on to each other. You are my best friend and make me laugh every day just by being you. Kevy D, I am amazed that every day I love you more, and I look forward to spending many years together. You are such a humble man and have such a heart for the hurting. You are my treasure.

Emilee: You are a wonderful daughter. There is no other little girl on earth I love and adore more than you. You have grown to be such a beautiful lady, and I'm so proud of you. In so many ways, you held me together when I was sad, protected me when I doubted myself, and made me crack up laughing when I thought my joy was gone. I'm crazy about you and admire your strength. Words can't express how much I love you.

Dr. William E. Anderson (Pastor Bill): Thank you for investing in and encouraging my family and me on our journey. No matter how busy life got, you were never too busy to care for your sheep—even the crippled lambs. In my darkest hours you loved and encouraged me. You met me where I was but never allowed me to stay in the pit. You and Addie have been a priceless treasure in our lives. You have helped me grow and instilled in me a deep desire to know more of Christ Jesus. Through the years, you told me that this story needed to be shared because it truly shows the thumbprint of God. Thank you for loving a crushed mother. I am eternally grateful for the love, guidance, and encouragement you have given me all along the way. Now that my wounds have been healed, you have given me the courage to share my scars. My prayer is that all who are hurting find someone who will lead them to the Great Physician, Jesus Christ, my healer.

From Tyler Sexton:

First, we thank our Lord and Savior, Jesus Christ, without whom our hope would be lost and this testimony not even possible.

There are so many who have encouraged us along the way through this long process, and we are truly grateful for all your love and prayers. Our prayer is that God will bless the lives of those who are overwhelmed and have dim hopes for the future. We pray that they may see how an ordinary family with broken hearts, dreams, and lives laid everything at the cross, and then God did the extraordinary.

> O Lord, You are my God;
> I will exalt You, I will give thanks to Your name;
> For You have worked wonders,
> Plans formed long ago, with perfect faithfulness.
>
> ISAIAH 25:1, NASB

I want to dedicate this to all the children with special needs I've been privileged to mentor and serve though the years. You are more than conquerors! Kids like you are the reason my mother and I have written this book and the reason that I entered the career of medicine. You represent my entire goal in my developing career. It will be an honor to help you in the future and many more patients just like you! Thank you!

Laura: My beautiful and loving wife, it's hard to believe that on January 2008 we arrived on an island that few people even knew existed. I set out to become a doctor, and God gave me so much more than that. I could have never planned for what God was going to give me while on the island of Saint Eustatius. God used Statia and one of the most faith-cultivating journeys of my life to introduce me to you! You're my best friend, and words can't express how much I love and care for you. Together we will be vessels of God's service in accordance with His plan, so that in all areas of our lives, Christ will have the preeminence and glory. Throughout the pressures of the present and the uncertainties of the future, I promise to be faithful to you as we continue this great adventure under Christ's guidance.

Harper Grace: My most precious gift is that God allows me to be your earthly father. May you always know the miracle that you are and how special, beautiful, and incredible you are. I pray that I will be a father who guides you to the arms of the greatest Father you can ever know—Christ. And I pray you see the love I have for you as unending and everlasting.

My Father, Kevin: You are my hero, the greatest man. Your sacrifices on my behalf have never gone unnoticed, and treasures in heaven have been stored up for you. You have shown me the attributes of a real man, a man of God. I love you! It's with the greatest pride that I have the privilege to call you my earthly father.

My Sister, Emilee: Sib, your excitement and loyalty are beyond compare. I'm blessed to have a sister such as you. Throughout the years, you've been one of my greatest supporters, protectors, and admirers. For that, I thank you and love you deeply.

Sweet Potato: Thank you for all the love and support you have shown me. Our connection is even more than that of a mother and son; it's a deep adoration. Thank you for knowing where the true hope lies and for letting me pursue hopes and dreams instead of a miraculous physical cure, for you knew where the miracles originate. Thank you for always being in my corner, comforting and encouraging me, and for teaching me that all is possible with the Lord. I love you!

Notes

CHAPTER 6: FACING MY REAL LIFE

1. "Americans with Disabilities: 2010," US Census Bureau, 2012, https://www.census.gov/newsroom/releases/archives/miscellaneous/cb12-134.html.
2. "Americans with Disabilities: 2010," US Census Bureau.

CHAPTER 7: BEYOND DESPERATION

1. "Depression," National Institute of Mental Health, February 2018, https://www.nimh.nih.gov/health/topics/depression/index.shtml.

CHAPTER 11: THE GREAT PHYSICIAN

1. Vernon J. Bourke, ed., *The Essential Augustine* (Indianapolis, IN: Hackett, 1947), 196.
2. *The Good Doctor*, "Burnt Food," season 1, episode 1, directed by Seth Gordon, written by David Shore, performed by Freddie Highmore, Nicholas Gonzalez, and Antonia Thomas (Burbank, CA: ABC, 2017), https://abc.go.com/shows/the-good-doctor/episode-guide/season-1/01-pilot-burnt-food.

About the Authors

TYLER SEXTON serves as chair of pediatrics and as a physician in hyperbaric medicine and wound care at Singing River Hospital in Pascagoula, Mississippi.

Since 2003, Tyler has also been an international motivational speaker, raising awareness about the adversity faced by people with disabilities and encouraging an attitude of achievement regardless of the disability or situation. He also mentors children with disabilities.

He's been featured in numerous books, articles, and radio and television broadcasts, including ABC's *20/20*, *The 700 Club*, *The God Squad*, *Hour of Power*, *The Helpline,* and the Focus on the Family broadcast.

Tyler works with special interest groups, educating them in the field of hyperbaric medicine, and treats countless individuals suffering from decompression illness in the United States and abroad. He also specializes in bringing hyperbaric medical clinics to underserved parts of the world.

He's an American College of Hyperbaric Medicine-approved training provider and the vice president of the American College of Hyperbaric Medicine. He's also a member of the American Professional Wound Care Association and has achieved the status of "Master," a designation recognizing key opinion leaders who have positively influenced wound care through education, research, and advocacy.

In addition to being a certified hyperbaric wound specialist, a certified hyperbaric technologist, and a diver medic technician, Tyler also holds certificates of added qualification in hyperbaric medicine and wound care by the American Board of Wound Healing.

LISA SEXTON has been featured on *Hour of Power*, *The 700 Club*, and *The Helpline*, and has also contributed to the *Focus on the Family* magazine. In her writing as well as her speaking engagements, Lisa offers a mother's personal insight about having a child with disabilities. From the initial fears of pregnancy to the heartache of being told your child isn't "perfect," Lisa addresses the blessings of motherhood and the challenges all mothers face on different levels.